1987

Child Support in America

Child Support in America

Practical Advice for Negotiating—and Collecting—a Fair Settlement

JOSEPH I. LIEBERMAN

Yale University Press · New Haven and London

Designed by Nancy Ovedovitz and set in Times Roman type by Eastern Graphics. Printed in the United States of America by Halliday Lithograph Corporation, West Hanover, Massachusetts

Library of Congress Cataloging-in-Publication Data

Lieberman, Joseph I.
   Child support in America.
   Bibliography: p.
   Includes index.
   1. Child support—Law and legislation—United States.
  2. Child support—United States. I. Title.
   KF549.L54   1986   346.7301′72   86-5501
   ISBN 0-300-03693-0 (alk. paper)   347.306172

The paper in this book meets the guidelines for permanence and durability of the Committee on Production Guidelines for Book Longevity of the Council on Library Resources.

10   9   8   7   6   5   4   3   2   1

I dedicate this book to my father, Henry Lieberman, who was born on April 3, 1915, and died on January 3, 1986. It is altogether fitting that this book about what can be done to force delinquent fathers to support their children be dedicated to a man who was the embodiment of what a responsible father should be. For my two sisters and me, my father was a strong and unwavering source of financial, psychological, moral, and spiritual support. We miss him dearly.

Contents

Preface

> The duty of parents to provide for the maintenance of their children, is a principle of natural law; an obligation . . . laid on them not only by nature herself but by their own proper act, in bringing them into the world; for they would be in the highest manner injurious to their issue, if they only gave their children life that they might afterwards see them perish.
>
> Sir William Blackstone,
> *Commentaries on the Law of England in Four Books*

This is a book with a bias, but a bias based in fact. Child support in America is a national disgrace. There is no more widespread and profoundly consequential example of lawlessness in our society today than fathers' refusal to care for their children after divorce. More than half of the fathers who have been ordered by the court to pay child support disobey these orders.[1] More than 2 million mothers are owed a total of nearly $4 billion by delinquent fathers.[2] The numbers are worse for fathers of children on welfare. Only 10.2 percent of them support their children; for the federal fiscal year ending September 30, 1983, such fathers failed to pay more than $5 billion in support obligations incurred during that year.[3]

Unless American citizens take action, the problem will worsen. The traditional family unit of father, mother, and children has been shattered. More than 8.4 million women with children live in a household in which the natural father is not present.[4] Each year the states assume the burden of collection in 500,000 new child-support obligations that are established in nonwelfare and welfare cases.[5]

As attorney general of Connecticut, I represent the interests of the people of my state in various areas, including environmental protection, consumer protection, and antitrust cases. Collections work is normally one of the least appealing assignments a lawyer can be given. I have therefore been surprised to find that one of the most compelling facets of my work is the collection of child support owed by fathers to their children, ex-spouses, and the state. I have seen the extraordinary extent of neglect by fathers and the impact this has on the lives of their children and ex-wives. It is difficult to review individual case files without becoming angry. Fathers who can pay are not paying. They are not meeting the obligation that they have agreed to meet or that has been ordered by a court. As a result, their fellow taxpayers pay, their children suffer, and their ex-wives struggle to stay economically afloat. In fact, the failure of delinquent fathers to pay child support is the major reason why more than half the American families that are headed by a woman live below the poverty level.

This is the context in which I have written this book. I have three goals. The first is to present a plain language guide to the law of child support for lawyers, judges, family counselors, state officials, and others who work with divorcing couples. The second is to give those couples themselves a basic understanding of the rules of the legal world they have entered, so that those who are not receiving the amount of support for their children that they deserve can learn how to correct that situation.

My third goal is to describe the current system of child support enforcement, explain why it does not work, and offer proposals to improve it. I hope that this part of the book will provide a charter for action by those who are owed child support and those who care about them.

I begin chapter 1 with a brief historical overview of the way in which our legal system has allocated the responsibility for child support, from seventeenth-century England to the tough new law adopted by Congress in 1984. In chapter 2, I describe the crisis we face today in enforcing child support orders, analyze the reasons for the rampant paternal delinquency, and detail the effect it has on mothers, children, and taxpayers.

Chapters 3 to 5 present guidelines on how to avoid becoming a victim of nonsupport. Chapter 3 focuses on the negotiation of an adequate child support agreement. Chapter 4 discusses ways to increase the amount of child support one is receiving, and chapter 5 explains what can be done by a person who is not receiving the child support her ex-spouse has been ordered to pay.

Chapter 6 presents a plan of action for improving the system by legislative, administrative, and judicial reforms. In appendix A, I have provided the names and addresses of the agencies responsible for enforcing child support laws in the fifty states, and in B a list of the citizen-advocacy groups that are working to change them, so that readers who wish to become more involved in bringing about either personal improvement or programmatic reform can more easily do so.

A final word about reality and nomenclature. Although joint child custody arrangements after divorce are invited by the laws of an increasing number of states and decreed by a growing number of judges, they still apply to a small minority—no more than 15 percent of postdivorce families. Some fathers have custody of their children after divorce and share or receive support from their former wives, but the norm continues to be that mothers receive custody and fathers owe child support. Therefore, throughout this book, I use the words *mother* and *ex-wife* to describe the custodial parent who is owed child support and the words *father* and *ex-husband* to describe the noncustodial parent who must pay child support.

I can think of no more jarring example of disrespect for the law than the failure of fathers to meet their responsibility to their children. As Blackstone suggested, this responsibility was thought to be so fundamental that it was part of the natural law, the instinctive order of existence. Apparently that has changed now, and since it has, the law that we write and enforce must intervene aggressively to restore respect for what is truly natural and right. That is what this book is about and what I hope it will help engender.

Acknowledgments

I want to thank Joseph Dumond, Richard Kehoe, and Margaret Frederick Valentino for their invaluable and selfless help in preparing this book.

I am also grateful to my friends at the Yale University Press, Tina Weiner, Gladys Topkis, and Alexander Metro, for their encouragement and guidance.

I thank my wife, Hadassah Freilich Lieberman, for urging me to write this book, for creatively reviewing its contents, for understanding the time I had to spend working on it, and for being such a wonderful wife and partner.

Finally, Hadassah and I acknowledge our children, Matthew and Rebecca Lieberman and Ethan Tucker, for demanding so much of our support and for being so worthy of it.

CHAPTER ONE

Child Support Laws: A Brief History

ENGLISH ORIGINS

The origin of our child support laws, as of so much else in our legal system, is in England. The historical development of these laws mirrors society's changing sense of the "appropriate" relationship between husbands and wives and between parents and their children. The beginning point is expressed in Blackstone's classic observation that "the husband and wife are one person in law; that is, the very being or legal existence of the woman is suspended during the marriage, or at least is incorporated and consolidated into that of the husband."[1] In this view of what was "appropriate" the husband enjoyed a form of ownership of both wife and children. With that possession went responsibility. Fathers had a moral obligation to support their children, just as children had a moral obligation to provide labor for their fathers. In this closed agricultural unit, every member of the family had a functional role. The father was dominant but also accountable.

> The wants and weaknesses of childhood render maintenance by someone other than the child himself indispensable, and the voice of nature indicates the parent, that is the father, as the fittest person to afford it.[2]

The father's authority and responsibility were so well accepted that if the couple separated it was the *father* who usually received custody and, with it, the obligation to support his children.

> The child, helpless in extreme infancy and required in the mature years of its minority to obey the reciprocal duty of serving its parents, is not de-

1

prived of its natural and legal right of protection and support by its father because of any family quarrel or of any disagreement between husband and wife.[3]

Until early in the seventeenth century, the father's responsibility for his children was moral but not legal. Then, in 1601, the Elizabethan Poor Law was adopted, requiring that parents must provide basic support for their children. If they did not, the vote of two magistrates was enough to put them in jail, fine them, or seize their personal property to use for support of the children.

The common law provided two other remedies for nonsupport. The first was criminal. If the prosecutor could prove that a child was injured by his father's failure to care for him, the father was guilty of a common-law misdemeanor. Second, a person who had given "necessaries," such as food, to the children could bring a lawsuit against the father for the reasonable value of those goods or services. But merchants and other providers were understandably reluctant to provide "necessaries" to children who lacked a visible and liable parent, so this common-law remedy was of little value. The children themselves could not sue their fathers because the English common law did not recognize minors as legally capable.

The father's obligation to support his children became more legally enforceable only when a nineteenth-century English court ruled that if a wife and husband separated because of his misconduct and the children lived with her, she could purchase "necessaries" for the children and he would be liable.[4]

Since the development of law usually mirrors the course of history, it is not surprising that the changes in family life brought on by the Industrial Revolution were reflected in the law of family relations. As fathers left the closed unit of the farm family and went to work in factories and offices, fundamental legal changes occurred. The mother became, and was recognized by the law as, the more influential force in the family home.[5] Although the father retained the appearance of dominance and ultimate financial responsibility, the mother was seen as the primary custodian of the children. The English Parliament recognized that change in 1839, when it decreed for the first time that a mother could be granted custody of a child under the age of seven.

AMERICAN VARIATIONS

Nineteenth-century American courts, for reasons of equity as well as because of the presumption that maternal care was better for the children, reflected that same movement away from the father's absolute right of custody:

> American courts were more likely to look at the circumstances and facts of the particular case and to rely on fault or evidence of parental unfitness. Since social convention customarily led to the wife's filing for and being awarded the divorce as the innocent party, and since the fault-based custody standard assumed that children would be best taken care of by the innocent party, the court's reliance on fault as evidence of parental unfitness was more likely to result in a large proportion of maternal custody awards.[6]

These trends were formalized by American courts during the early twentieth century, when they adopted the "tender years" presumption, which held that children were especially dependent on a mother's love and caring during their earlier years. While American statutory law had established a neutral ideal of "the best interests of the child" as the standard for child custody decisions, American courts had continued to award custody to the mother unless there was clear evidence that she was unfit.

The law's conception of what was "natural" had changed. The mother was now preferred to the father. As an American judge wrote,

> The preference for the mother needs no argument to support it because it arises out of the very nature and instincts of motherhood; nature has ordained it.[7]

Remaining constant through all the changing perceptions of family roles, however, was the father's responsibility to support his children. Although early twentieth-century American courts refused to recognize the father's interest in his children as possessions or his absolute right to their labor, they increasingly recognized his legal responsibility to provide for the children after divorce. The general acceptance of that rule was based in part on the assumption that women had less capacity to earn money. But it was also applied when the woman had assets or income, presumably because the father's responsibility for his children had risen to the level of accepted morality, regardless of economics.[8]

In time, every American state encoded this paternal obligation by making nonsupport a criminal misdemeanor and providing a variety of civil remedies, including attaching the father's property, garnishing his wages, and holding him in contempt when he did not support his children.

The recent revolution in women's role in the family and society has also brought about legal changes, although with ironic and imperfect results. Once the states began to reflect these changes during the early 1970s by adopting state equal rights amendments, it was inevitable that men would challenge their unequal, that is, greater, legal responsibility to support their children. The first test came in Pennsylvania in 1974, when a father, contesting the child support order a court had imposed on him, said it was beyond his financial capacity. He argued that the order had been issued with no consideration of the mother's relative economic ability, but simply because he was a man. Therefore, he contended, the support order was unconstitutional. The Pennsylvania court agreed, declaring that "a presumption that the father, solely because of his sex, . . . must accept the principal burden of financial support of minor children . . . is clearly a vestige of the past and incompatible with present recognition of equality of the sexes."[9] Since the best interest of the child should be the guiding standard in custody cases, the Pennsylvania court reasoned, the same standard should be applied to child support judgments. A child's interests are more likely to be protected if the financial capacities of both the mother and the father are considered in allocating responsibility. Two people could provide more support than one. This egalitarian norm was accepted in several other state court decisions and was incorporated in the Uniform Marriage and Divorce Act, which has thus far been adopted in eight states.

But the fact remains that the law's changing perspective on women did not alter the reflexive tendency of divorce courts to grant custody of children to mothers. And so mothers with custody have now been forced to fight some of the onerous results of legal and conceptual equality. Particularly important has been the contention, upheld by several courts, that state equal rights amendments do not require exact equality of contributions from mother and father but only a consideration by the judge of the financial capacity of each when allocating responsibility for child support. Equally critical has been the conclusion that the in-kind services of "caring for, supervising and maintaining" the children, which are usually provided by the mother, must be considered in setting child support.[10]

FEDERAL INTERVENTION

Because American family law has traditionally been the work of state legislators, judges, and administrators, the law of child support developed along independent but usually parallel paths in the fifty states. It was not until 1935 that the federal government became involved, and then only marginally, when, as part of the Social Security Act, it created the program of Aid to Families with Dependent Children (known as AFDC or, more popularly, as "welfare"). This program was created to limit the local community's historic responsibility for children whose parents had died or deserted them. It did so by sending money from Washington, via the states, to relatives of dependent children so that they might be cared for at home instead of in community institutions. While the original congressional concern was with children whose fathers had died, the AFDC program came to be used more frequently to help children whose fathers had left home and refused to pay support.

In 1949, the State of New York reacted to the problem of delinquent fathers by passing a law that allowed a mother or child to begin a lawsuit to collect support in the state where they lived and enforce it in the state where the child's father had gone. Within a year, ten other states adopted similar legislation, and the national Conference of Commissioners of Uniform Laws promulgated the Uniform Reciprocal Enforcement of Support Act (URESA). Eventually, every American state and territory adopted this law, which improved child support collections and naturally encouraged a similarity of child support enforcement procedures among the various jurisdictions. However, at best it provided an interstate collection mechanism. By itself it could not make child support files a priority for prosecutors. It did not offer any assistance to those children whose father had left home but remained in the same state. Nor, most important, could it keep pace with the dramatic demographic changes after World War II that cracked the traditional family unit, created more delinquent fathers, and put more and more children on welfare.

By fiscal year 1973, the AFDC program was costing the public $7.6 billion a year. Senator Russell Long of Louisiana echoed an increasingly popular sentiment when he asked in 1972: "Should our welfare system be made to support the children whose father cavalierly abandons them—or chooses not to marry the mother in the first place?"[11] The answer was a resounding no from a public that by the early 1970s had grown frustrated by the size of government and taxes and angry about the runaway fathers whose children the taxpayers were forced to support.

A congressional study issued in 1974 concluded:

> Eighty percent of AFDC children have absent parents, and almost one-third of these children are covered by support orders or agreements. However, although these orders represent findings that the parents are able to pay, few are obeyed.[12]

At about the same time, the RAND Corporation issued a report which showed that state welfare agencies were casual at best in trying to collect child support from the fathers of children on welfare. The RAND report also concluded that many of those fathers could afford to pay.

Such convincing documentation combined with the growing public fury over welfare costs to produce an irresistible force. The result was the Child Support and Establishment of Paternity Act of 1974, which created Title IV-D of the Social Security Act, aimed at cutting the cost of welfare by stimulating the states to go after delinquent fathers. If a state's child support enforcement effort (known thereafter as its IV-D agency) did not meet federal standards, Washington would reduce its contribution to the state's AFDC budget by 5 percent, a multimillion-dollar penalty in most instances. If a state's child support collection program was approved, the federal government would pay 75 percent of its cost. The new law also required applicants for AFDC to assign their child support collection rights to the state and to cooperate in locating the fathers of their children.

Each state was required to establish a parent locator service which would review public records of all kinds in pursuit of wayward fathers. If unsuccessful, the state IV-D agency could then call on the Federal Parent Locator Service, which would search federal data banks, including the Internal Revenue Service and Social Security Administration. Working with the state's attorney general, the IV-D agency would go to court to establish paternity (if that was necessary), obtain a court order of support, and enforce that order either in the court of the mother's state, or, through URESA, in the court of the state where the father had gone.

In an unusually farsighted provision, Congress made all the collection services of the IV-D program available, for a very small fee, to mothers of children who were not on welfare. The logic was that if these mothers did not receive child support from their children's father, they would eventually find themselves on welfare and cost the taxpayers a good deal more than the cost of collection services.

Although the 1974 legislation had popular support and was hailed by such authorities as Professor Harry Krause of the University of Illinois as "to date the most important federal legislative venture into family law,"[13] others initially opposed it. According to the League of Women Voters, for instance, the human and financial resources required to carry out the IV-D program would better be used "to strengthen family life and the welfare program in more constructive ways."[14] Even President Ford, in signing the bill, warned that "certain provisions of this legislation go too far by injecting the federal government into domestic relations."

However, experience with the new IV-D program quickly stifled the opposition. During its first full year of operation, fiscal year 1976, IV-D agencies throughout the United States collected $280 million in child support from AFDC fathers and $323 million from non-AFDC fathers, a total of $603 million. A year later the total was $818 million, and in 1978 it exceeded $1 billion for the first time ($472 million from AFDC fathers and $575 million from non-AFDC). In fiscal year 1983, the total reached almost $2 billion dollars ($1.1 billion non-AFDC and $880.2 million AFDC).

The human statistics are even more compelling. In 1978, the IV-D program located 453,620 absent fathers and established paternity in 110,714 cases. By 1983, those numbers had risen to 830,758 and 209,024, respectively.[15]

Although these results are certainly impressive, the national child support enforcement program was still not able to keep pace with the increasing disintegration of American families. The numerical proof of this disintegration is now sadly familiar. More than one million couples are divorced each year, and the result is that more than 500,000 children need support from a noncustodial parent. The number of children born out of wedlock and living out of wedlock soared from 527,000 in 1970 to 1,745,000 in 1980 to 2,800,000 in 1982. These children require support from either their fathers or the government. More than 90 percent of current AFDC families receive support because one of the parents has abandoned the family and left the children unsupported.[16]

The cumulative child support debt is staggering. More than $4 billion of support is owed by fathers to their children, money that cannot be used to offset the suffering of mothers and children described in the next chapter. In recent years, those numbers also have found political expression as child support came to be perceived and acted upon as "a woman's issue." Anger toward delinquent fathers of children on welfare, which stimulated the national legislation of 1974, continued to move people in the 1980s; it was augmented by a realization that mothers who were not on welfare were also owed child support by higher-income-earning fathers, and that child support delinquency was the most important reason why poverty in America had been "feminized."

Because of the increasing political importance of the women's vote, the child support situation provided an invitation to action. Child support enforcement became a priority for woman's political action groups. Throughout America, mothers who were owed child support created organizations to make their plight visible and to lobby for legislative and administrative changes.

The reaction came first from state governments that adopted new laws to seize unemployment benefits and state tax refunds owed to delinquent fathers and direct them instead to meeting their child support obligations. Most attention was focused on laws that would ensure payment of child support by making it easier to have money deducted automatically from the paychecks of delinquent fathers.

In Connecticut, for example, in 1983 I asked the legislature to authorize an automatic deduction from the wages of a father who was more than thirty days late in paying child support. Our early experience with this new law has been very encouraging. During 1984, when the automatic deduction system went into effect, collections rose more than 20 percent, bringing in an additional $11 million.

That result and similar results in other states are worth noting because a thirty-day automatic deduction program is the heart of the new federal child support legislation adopted by Congress during the summer of 1984. Cosponsored by Democratic congresswoman Barbara Kennelly of Connecticut and Republican congresswoman Margaret Roukema of New Jersey and supported by the Reagan administration, this legislation is the most important change in child support law since the IV-D program was created in 1974. All states are now required to provide automatic wage deductions after thirty days of delinquency, to extend the statute of limitations for paternity actions to eighteen years, to accelerate judicial and administrative processing of child support cases, and to establish guidelines for the use of judges and other officials responsible for establishing child support orders.

I have tried in this brief history to describe the mix of experiences that has brought the laws of child support to where they are today. A mother trying to collect child support or an assistant attorney general working to enforce a child support order must operate within a legal system that is derived from old English common law, encoded in nationally promulgated uniform laws, and strengthened by the growing involvement of the state and national governments. Although there has never been a wider awareness of the problem of child support enforcement or a broader consensus favoring action, the extent of delinquency still outstrips the legal system's ability to collect.

New laws may help, but the problem will remain and perhaps even worsen, since demographic projections show that when we enter the twenty-first century barely half the children in America will spend their entire childhood with their natural parents. Unless there is a change in our society's value system so that we no longer hold fathers accountable for their children, the problem of child support enforcement will be with us for a long time.

In the next chapter, I will describe the problem in more detail, analyzing which fathers do pay and which do not, why they behave the way they do, and what effect their nonpayment has on mothers, children, and taxpayers.

CHAPTER TWO

The Current Crisis in Child Support

Let me begin with the sad statistical litany of family disintegration and paternal neglect according to the Bureau of the Census:[1]

- From 1970 to 1981, the number of divorces in America doubled.
- From 1970 to 1981, the number of children living with only one parent increased by 54 percent to 12.6 million, one of every five children in America.
- Of the 4 million women who were owed child support in 1981, only 47 percent received the full amount due, and 28 percent received absolutely nothing; the aggregate amount of child support payments due in 1981 was $9.9 billion, but only $6.1 billion was actually received.
- From 1970 to 1981, the average amount of child support received by mothers rose from $1,800 to $2,110 per child, but after adjusting for inflation, the payments actually decreased by 16 percent in real terms.
- In 1982, only 15 percent of divorced or separated women were awarded alimony, and only 43 percent of those women actually received full payment of the alimony they were owed, meaning that child support is the only form of assistance most divorced women can expect from their ex-husbands.
- Between 1970 and 1981, the number of people in families below the poverty level that were headed by women *rose* by 54 percent, while the number of male-headed poor families *decreased* by 50 percent.
- In 1981, women headed almost 50 percent of all the poor families in America.

The figures above should be read more than once. Their cumulative effect is powerful. Increasing numbers of women are heading households and caring for children, but they are not receiving the child support payments owed by the father of those children, so more and more of them are falling into poverty.

Let me now try to answer some questions about child support awards that emerge naturally from these statistics.

WHO DECIDES ON THE AMOUNT OF CHILD SUPPORT?

Child support awards are ultimately the work of state judges. Although every state's statutes set out general standards that a judge must consider in making an award, the judge is effectively on his own, and the judgments show it.

Kenneth White and R. Thomas Stone, Jr., studied the records of several Florida judges who handle child support cases and found that while each established a consistent pattern in his own decisions, there were wide variations among the judges in the awards they made in comparable factual circumstances.[2]

On the basis of a similar study of judicial decisions in Denver, Lucy Marsh Yee reported wide variations in child support awards, even by the same judge. In two cases decided under URESA, where the father's ability to pay and the child's needs are the only factors that can be considered, one judge ordered $50 per month in support for two children from a father with a net monthly income of $900 but $120 a month for two children whose father earned $450.

Yee also found that in the cases studied, fathers were ordered to pay between 6 and 33 percent of their income to support one child and between 5.6 and 40 percent of their income to support two children.[3]

A random check of 150 of my office's files on cases with support orders entered between July 1, 1983, and June 30, 1984, illustrates the inconsistency of Connecticut judges in the award of child supports. For fathers earning between $145 and $155 a week, the court orders ranged from $10 a week to $60 a week for support for one child. The comparative range was not quite as great when the father was earning between $295 and $305 a week, but still considerable, going from $50 a week to $108 a week for support of one child. The variation in the support orders was approximately the same when orders were entered for two children.

Such gross variations invite the imposition of formulas that would regularize and equalize child support awards for parents and children in similar circumstances. Some jurisdictions have already promulgated child support tables; others are being pushed to do so by child support advocates and the new federal child support law.

Connecticut is currently experimenting with child support guidelines in two areas of the state, and the Connecticut legislature has mandated that guidelines be developed for use throughout the state by January 1, 1987. Obviously such guidelines are sorely needed, but the results in states that have adopted them are mixed. Many judges resist standardization and protect their prerogative to react subjectively to the particular case before them. One Pennsylvania judge put it this way:

> The guidelines greatly oversimplify many issues. . . . You will have to make so many exceptions . . . that soon you will have no rule. The ideal judge in these matters uses a common law, rather than a Napoleonic Code approach. . . . As for the new guidelines . . . they are so inconsistent with the Superior Court cases that judges will not be able to make much use of them. While I get money from the IV-D program, I get my law from the Superior Court.[4]

In fact, one study done in Los Angeles County showed that judges were generally ordering support at levels below the recommended schedule, perhaps because they erroneously viewed the schedule as a maximum.[5]

In spite of the disparities in individual child support awards, there seems to be a remarkable, unconscious agreement about the maximum percentage of a father's income that a judge will ask him to pay to support his children. As Lenore J. Weitzman points out in her classic study of the economic consequences of divorce: "A man is rarely ordered to part with more than a third of his net income, no matter what his income level."[6] Her analysis of child support awards in California also shows that the higher a father's income, the lower the percentage he will be ordered to pay in child support.

Men with net incomes of over $50,000 annually paid only 5 percent in child support, while those who made between $10,000 and $30,000 paid 25 percent, and those with incomes below $10,000 were ordered to pay 37 percent of that amount in child support. The fact that higher-income men are more likely to pay alimony partially explains the variance, but only partially, because very few women (approximately 15 percent of all who are divorced) receive alimony. The difference also suggests that judges have in mind a fixed amount of support per child regardless of the income of the father or the life-style expenses of the mother and children.

CAN FATHERS AFFORD TO PAY
CHILD SUPPORT AWARDS?

"Yes" is the answer given by every study of child support that I have seen. David Chambers, for instance, found that 80 percent of the Michigan fathers he studied could maintain themselves very comfortably if they paid the full amount of child support they owed.[7] Weitzman concluded that almost three-fourths of the California fathers in her study could pay the appropriate support without reducing their standard of living.

A special indicator of fathers' ability to pay child support was used by two Michigan economists, Saul Hoffman and John Holmes, who compared household income and needs of men and women after divorce. They found that the fiscal condition of the men *improved* 17 percent while the women's economic capacity *decreased* by 29 percent.[8] Weitzman applied the Hoffman–Holmes formula to her data from California and came up with an even more bruising result. One year after divorce, the women were 73 percent *worse* off while the fathers were 42 percent *better* off.

Although wealthier men are usually ordered to pay a smaller percentage of their income in child support, this does not mean that they are more likely to pay it. Weitzman's study concluded that fathers in California with annual incomes between $30,000 and

$50,000 had as high a probability of child support delinquency as those with incomes of less than $10,000.

From her analysis of fathers in Denver, Yee provides dramatic proof of fathers' ability to pay. Two-thirds of the men paid more in monthly installments for their cars than in monthly payments for their children. In only one out of five cases that went to trial did a judge order child support higher than car payments. One man, with a net income of $1,000 per month and car payments of $211 per month, was ordered to pay only $100 monthly to support his two children.

Yee concluded that even "though the law indicates that the ability of the father to pay and the needs of the children should be the only issues in a URESA [support] case," in fact the father's capacity is "not the determinative factor" and the children's needs "receive virtually no consideration."

In short, not only are child support awards fair in relationship to fathers' ability to pay but there is reason to believe that most fathers could pay more. Then, why don't they pay?

WHY DON'T FATHERS PAY CHILD SUPPORT?

Although the studies I have quoted show that most fathers can afford to pay child support, they also show that some cannot, perhaps because they are unemployed or psychologically disabled. For this minority of fathers, the answer to our question is simple and fiscal. They do not pay because they do not have the money. Recent research suggests, as we shall see below, that while economic factors are the direct cause of nonpayment by these fathers, emotional problems are also at the origins of their failure to care for their children.

But what motivates the rest of the fathers—the majority—who fail to support their children for noneconomic reasons? Social scientists have been working recently to provide answers to that question. Both Judith Wallerstein and Dorothy Huntington are on the staff of

the Center for the Family in Transition at Corte Madera, California.
From 1971 to 1977, they studied 60 divorcing, mostly white and
middle-class California couples and their 131 children. Although
their Marin County sample was not totally representative of the national population, their findings offer the most comprehensive and
sometimes surprising data available about the noneconomic factors
that cause fathers not to pay child support.[9]

Wallerstein and Huntington found that the following factors were
not causally related to nonsupport.

1. *Educational attainment*. Some of the fathers who were most neg-
   ligent in their payments had graduate degrees.
2. *Relationship with ex-wife*. There was no significant correlation
   between payment of child support and the cordiality of relations
   with the ex-wife. "People who were friendly or feuding were as
   likely or unlikely to provide economic support for their children," the authors concluded.
3. *Circumstances of ex-wife*. The ex-wife's physical and mental
   health had no special influence on whether the father paid, even
   in cases where the father had been an involved parent during the
   marriage and had been concerned about leaving his children with
   a sick mother.
4. *Remarriage*. Remarriage of the father or mother, or cohabitation
   of either with another, did not determine the level of the father's
   payments.
5. *Predivorce relationship with children*. There was no significant
   link between the quality of a father's relationship with his children prior to the divorce and his support of them after the divorce.

Factors that Wallerstein and Huntington found do correlate with
nonsupport are as follows:

1. *The father's psychological intactness*. There was a much higher
   correlation between the psychological stability of the father and

the payment of support than between his economic stability and support payments. Wallerstein and Huntington found a high incidence of alcoholism and "disabling psychological dysfunction" among fathers who gave little or no support.

2. *The ex-wife's economic status.* Women who were economically successful after divorce were much less likely to receive the child support they were owed by their ex-husbands. The reverse, however, was not always true. A woman's economic difficulties did not necessarily encourage her ex-husband to greater fidelity in support payments.

3. *Children of remarriage.* While remarriage itself did not affect child support payments, the presence of stepchildren or the birth of natural children in the father's remarriage were clearly associated with lower payments to the children of his former marriage. That was the result regardless of whether the father was financially capable of supporting the children of both marriages.

4. *Visitation and postdivorce relationship with children.* Here the results were mixed and changed over time. Denial of visitation rights did not directly correlate with failure to make child support payments, but the relationship between visits by the father with his children and payment of child support became much more important over time. In other words, at the end of the five-year study, fathers who had regular, satisfactory visits with their children were much more likely to pay support.

The work of Wallerstein and Huntington provides explanations but not excuses for paternal nonsupport. So long as a father is financially able to pay, there is no acceptable excuse. Chambers, for instance, ultimately attributes fathers' failure to support their children to a more general human condition: "There are few identifiable groups so self-motivated toward payments that they pay as well as they are able without threat."[10] Chambers' answer to our question, then, is that fathers do not pay because they do not want to pay and the system does not force them to pay. His study showed that tougher enforcement procedures, including the jailing of delinquent fathers and direct deduction of child support payments from a father's wages, would lead to better payment records.

Weitzman agrees that enforcement is the key. She points out that although California had tough child support laws during the late 1970s, when she completed her study, "attorneys and judges are reluctant to use them." In her random sample of child support cases during 1977, Weitzman found that fewer than 5 percent were secured by a wage attachment.

This has been the norm nationally. Since state judges have been at the center of the American child support system, they are inevitably part of the explanation of fathers' failure to pay. For too long, state judges did not take child support cases seriously, hesitated to order adequate amounts of support, and then refused to punish those men who did not pay.

The attitude of one family judge in New York City, as described by a former city Human Resources administrator is revealing and all too representative.[11] During the summer of 1978, the administrator Blanche Bernstein, troubled by low collections of child support awards, visited the Brooklyn Family Court of Judge Philip D. Roache, where she found a stubborn resistance to ordering fathers to pay more and a shocking ignorance of the fact that many delinquent fathers could pay child support but simply chose not to. The judge revealed "a lack of sympathy with the IV-D program" and complained to Administrator Bernstein with three questions, each of which was based on a mistaken factual premise:

- "What is the point of bringing in all these 18- or 19-year-olds who have not seen their fathers for 15 years to try to establish paternity?" (Most paternity cases concern younger children.)
- "What is the use of bringing their fathers into court since they are all on public assistance?" (Most were not.)
- "What is the use of bringing these men in for support since none of them is earning very much?" (Most were earning enough to contribute something.)

When Bernstein asked the judge why he consistently ordered support at levels below the standard established by the State of New York, he said that he "knew better what a man could afford to contribute to the support of his child."

Bernstein attributes judicial weakness in enforcing child support laws to judges' jealous protection of their discretionary powers. She explains: "Each judge tends to regard himself in the image of Solomon. Limits to his discretion are considered not only as a diminution of his power and authority but demeaning to his status." She also blames the "liberal, humanitarian tradition" that prevailed in judicial appointments in New York City and State and resulted in "an over-reaction to past and existing discriminations against minorities, materializing in . . . lower expectations with regard to parental responsibility among low-income families."

If "humanitarianism" has been a cause of judicial softness in child support decisions, as Blanche Bernstein believed, its effect has changed in recent years with the growing awareness of the impact that paternal delinquency has on the lives of mothers and children. Humanitarian concern has been redirected to the mother and has led to a public outcry against the status quo that has begun to reach the ears of the judiciary. Throughout the country, judges are beginning to act more aggressively to compel fathers to support their children.

WHAT EFFECT DOES THE FATHER'S FAILURE TO PAY CHILD SUPPORT HAVE ON THE MOTHER?

Child support, as its name makes clear, is ordered for the benefit of children. But since most children who do not live with both parents live with the mother, and since very few mothers receive alimony, the failure of fathers to make child support payments has a disastrous effect on the fiscal health of mothers.

Even if more fathers paid child support, their ex-wives would suffer because child support awards are generally not consistent with the real cost of raising children, which the mother, as the custodial

parent, must pay. Judges tend to base the amount of child support
they order on a conservative estimate of what the father can pay.
They are more concerned with the father's ability to continue to live
adequately than with what it actually costs to raise children. They
consider income more than costs. Several Los Angeles judges interviewed by Lenore Weitzman referred to welfare and remarriage
as "preferable solutions" to saddling some former husbands with
greater support obligations.[12]

When Weitzman compared child support awards with standardized estimates of the cost of raising children, she found that the
average support award did not cover half of the actual cost. Such a
discrepancy naturally compounds the mother's problems because the
child lives with her. She is forced to pay whatever is not covered by
the child support award. Because the woman is almost always the
less financially able spouse, the inadequacy of child support awards
deepens her fiscal plight and increases the inequity of the system.
The less able partner is forced to pay more. That twisted result
grows worse over time because child-rearing costs escalate with
inflation while most child support awards remain constant. In some
cases (only 10 percent of child support awards in Weitzman's study)
there is a built-in escalator tied to cost-of-living increases; in a relatively small number of other cases, wives can afford to hire a lawyer
to return to court to try to increase their awards.

Our discussion thus far has assumed that the father is meeting his
child support obligation but that the amount is inadequate. We know
that more than half the fathers in America do not meet even that
obligation.

In their study of 60 middle-class divorcing couples in California,
Wallerstein and Huntington found that only 20 percent of the women
were financially secure five years after divorce. One-third of them
"were engaged in a daily struggle for survival, including chronic
worry over meeting monthly bills." Seven percent had gone onto the
welfare rolls. Although only 34 percent of the women had worked
while married, 75 percent were employed five years after divorce.
The authors add, however, that "many of the working women were

frustrated with their poor earnings and sought in vain to improve their financial position."[13]

A 1979 Department of Labor study found that 58.9 percent of married women with children but no husband present and 63 percent of unmarried mothers had jobs.[14] In reviewing these data, the U.S. Commission on Civil Rights has concluded that "increased labor force participation has not translated into increased economic security." The reasons given are poor child support payments and continuing discrimination against women in employment and compensation.[15]

The burden grows heavier the higher the family's income was before divorce. Weitzman puts it this way:

> Divorced men have much more money to spend on themselves than their former wives at every level of predivorce family income. Where the discrepancy is smallest, in lower income families, the husband and every member of his post divorce family [have] almost twice as much money as his former wife and every member of her postdivorce family (who are typically his children).[16]

In families with annual predivorce incomes of $40,000 or more, Weitzman found an "enormous" gap. The wife and children have to live at 48 percent of their previous income level while the husband has *200 percent* of his former financial capacity. The result is that the poverty rate for all female householders in 1981 was more than three times that for male householders and more than five times that of intact families.[17]

In sum, divorce without adequate child support payments is a financial disaster for most women.

WHAT EFFECT DOES THE FATHER'S FAILURE TO PAY CHILD SUPPORT HAVE ON THE CHILD?

Reports of the California divorcing couples and their children who were studied by Judith Wallerstein and her associates Joan Kelly and Dorothy Huntington from 1971 to 1977 provide us with the most objective answer to the question of how paternal neglect of support payments affects children.

The first and most obvious answer is that less support makes the children poorer. More concealed are the noneconomic consequences of nonsupport. For example, newly divorced mothers are usually forced to go to work while continuing to keep house and bring up their children and also trying to begin a social life. Thus they have less time to spend with their children at a period when the children probably need them most because of their father's absence. Twenty-five percent of the mothers interviewed by Wallerstein and Kelly said that within six months of separation they were "substantially less available to their children."[18]

Lower income also often forces mothers to move to a less expensive house or apartment in a new neighborhood, thus breaking their children's existing relationships with friends and schoolmates. Wallerstein and Kelly found that during the first three years of divorce, "almost two-thirds of the children had changed their place of residence, and a substantial number moved three or more times."

Most children face at least one such change sometime in their lives and adjust to it, but for many of the 131 children in the Wallerstein and Kelly study, the need to handle all these changes at once was more than they could effectively cope with. They felt abandoned and lost the general sense of stability they had before their parents separated.

In a later report on the same 60 families, Wallerstein and Huntington looked for specific links between a father's payment of child support and the psychological and social condition of his children. They concluded that good psychological adjustment among the children was significantly associated with adequate, stable child support, although poor psychological adjustment may be related to factors other than the issue of child support. In other words, most of the children who placed at the top of the researchers' scales of psychological, social, and academic performance were from families whose fathers regularly paid child support. But childhood depression and school performance below intellectual capacity occurred in children at every level of paternal support. The data also showed that the regularly supported children were much more likely to remain in the same residence and the same school, which may have been as much a cause of their psychological equilibrium as their fathers' finiancial payments.

It is worth noting that money alone was not enough to guarantee a well-adjusted child if it was not joined by regular contact with the father. Two of the children in the study never saw their father although he faithfully mailed child support payments to their mother in an envelope postmarked from a nearby community. "I have no feeling for my dad," the son angrily told interviewers. "It's like he's not my dad. He doesn't know me and I don't know him." Wallerstein and Huntington report:

> We were not surprised to learn that this very angry boy had been involved in several delinquent episodes and had experienced a stormy adolescence. . . . His sister was also profoundly troubled, preoccupied over the years with low self-esteem, suffering an acute sense of having been rejected, and a continuing intense anger that did not diminish over time.[19]

That is an extreme case but several other children in the study who were well supported but visited infrequently by their fathers "struggled for many years with anguish over their hurt and humiliation."

What is clear from all the data are the children's love for their father and their desire for *his* love regardless of whether he paid child support to their mother. One sixteen-year-old girl talked compassionately about her troubled father, who had never made support payments:

> He is my father and says he respects me and I believe him, and I believe also that he is very interested in me. . . . He should never have had a family. . . . Someday I will get a car and I will drive dad out to the ocean. He would like that. . . . Dad doesn't lie deliberately. . . . He just has such different impressions about so many things.[20]

Although this young woman's desire for her father's love is not unusual, her confidence about his respect is. Children who were badly supported were much more likely to suffer "intensely with the recurrent concern that their father did not love them," whereas children who were well supported were "significantly less likely to feel rejected by their father." In the typical case where the father was not faithful in paying support but nevertheless enjoyed an obviously comfortable life-style while the mother and children struggled, the children "were likely to be angry and depressed for many years and to remain preoccupied with this discrepancy in living standard."

The answer to the question we have posed is therefore complicated but clear in its meaning: a father's failure to pay child support will probably make his child psychologically, socially, and academically less stable.

CHAPTER THREE

How to Avoid Having a Child Support Problem

PRACTICING PREVENTIVE LAW

What can a divorcing couple do to avoid having a child support problem? The answer is: Negotiate a comprehensive child support agreement with each other or, if that is not possible, convince a judge to order a child support award that ensures that the children's standard of living will be as close as possible to what they would have enjoyed if the family had remained intact. In this chapter, I will offer a guide that can help achieve this happy result.

Because the facts presented thus far clearly reveal that mothers (and children and taxpayers) are most likely to be the victims of the current child support system, the advice in this chapter will be directed primarily to them. Fathers who want to support their children adequately will also find this chapter helpful as a guide to what should be included in a fair child-support agreement.

I hope that attorneys who practice family law will be able to use this chapter as a practical checklist of points to be covered and as a handy compilation of relevant case law.

THE JUDICIAL SETTING

Because judges decide how much child support is awarded and with what conditions and protections, much of the advice I offer in this chapter is based on the recorded opinion of judges.

But it is important to remember as you read about these judicial decisions that not more than 15 percent of divorces are actually ar-

gued out before a judge who writes the kind of opinions quoted in
this book. Most disputed issues of divorce are eventually resolved
out of court by the husband and wife and their lawyers, often with
the persuasion of a judge, who then records the results as a stipula-
tion or order of the court. But the rules that guide these out-of-court
negotiations between spouses and their attorneys and that establish
boundaries for their conclusions are the result of judicial decisions
and attorneys' speculation about how much support a judge is likely
to order in a particular situation.

What is most likely to move these judges? The studies cited in
chapter 2 show that judges have established no clearly discernible
pattern of logic for their child support awards. The range of awards
in cases involving families in similar circumstances is wide and inconsistent. In her study of child support awards in Denver, Lucy
Marsh Yee applied six objective factors to the awards and found that
none of them explained the differences. She concluded that judges
are affected more by the incomes of the father and mother than by
the costs of child rearing. Several of the studies I have quoted show
that judges establish in their own minds a maximum percentage of a
father's income in ordering child support. Weitzman, as noted,
found that limit to be about one-third of the father's income. The
"average" father in Yee's study was ordered to pay only 14.5 percent of his income for the support of one child and 18.6 percent for
the support of two children, even though guidelines promulgated by
the presiding judge of the Denver District Court required a father to
pay 20 percent of his income for one child and 34 percent for two
children.

In an address to a conference sponsored by the Domestic Relations Association of Pennsylvania in April 1977, Judge Charles
Sweet of Washington County, Pennsylvania, offered a refreshingly
candid reflection on how he and other judges decide child support
cases:

> The Superior Court . . . approaches the subject of support in an intellec-
> tually whimsical state of mind. In a 1973 case . . . the Superior Court
> said that it seems from the evidence that the wife and children are capable

of spending any amount the husband may be ordered to pay them. You will also note in reading such opinions . . . that most judicial time seems to be devoted to an analysis of the budget submitted by the husband and wife that each one's outlay is shown to be more than the income. . . . I disregard these budgets in large part . . . since they are largely untrustworthy. What I tell every other judge is to educate himself by doing the grocery shopping. You will remain out of touch with cost-of-living factors if you let your spouse or hired help do it. [1]

According to Judge Sweet, the "greatest virtue for a judge in these matters" is to be "predictable" because lawyers must know "approximately what is going to happen before a given judge on a given set of facts if protracted litigation, appeals, and enforcement actions are to be avoided." Nevertheless, Judge Sweet rejected the child support guidelines issued by the Pennsylvania Child Support Program as an oversimplification. "A table of percentages," he said, "could never work; the matter is far more sensitive than that, and the judge must from experience develop a feeling for practical amounts."

Although Judge Sweet's rhetoric may be less guarded than that of most jurists, his insistence on judical discretion is representative. The exercise of that discretion naturally produces varied results. Although specific child support awards by judges are inconsistent and confusing, the body of child support law that judges have developed, which underlies those awards, follows a discernible pattern and is the basis of the advice I offer.

CHOOSING A LAWYER

If a marriage is failing, it is time for the husband and wife to begin thinking about child support. If they have separated but not agreed on who will support the children, they are already late in learning what their rights are. Each should immediately find a lawyer by consulting friends who have gone through a divorce, calling the local bar association and asking for a list of lawyers who specialize in divorce cases, or looking at the attorneys' section of the telephone book. Divorce is usually an emotionally wrenching experience. Its economic results will probably determine for many years to come whether the divorcing couple can live comfortably. Therefore, the choice of a lawyer is very important. The husband and wife must find someone in whom each has confidence and whom each can afford. They should not hesitate to call several lawyers, ask about their fees, meet with them (even if that involves a consulting fee), and talk to people they have represented before deciding which lawyer to choose. Even if the initial steps of a divorce are amicable, neither spouse should be lulled into believing that he or she does not need an attorney.

OBTAINING TEMPORARY SUPPORT

Divorce is not an instantaneous process. It takes time—some required by legal procedures, some caused by court delays, and some because the spouses cannot agree on terms. The need for support, however, *is* usually instantaneous. That is why the immediate right to it is recognized by the law.

In most states, the right to seek an order of child support from a court begins on the day that divorce papers are served by one spouse on the other. Connecticut law, for instance, provides that "at any time after the return of a complaint . . . and after hearing, support *pendente lite* [while the case is pending before a final divorce decree is issued] may be awarded to either of the parties from the date of the filing of the application therefor." The Connecticut statute goes on to say that, in making an order for temporary support, the court must consider *all the factors enumerated* in the statute that governs the *permanent* awarding of child support. Although the order is temporary, the formula is the same. Even in states where there is not such a clear law, the power of courts to grant child support while the divorce arguments are proceeding is considered beyond question.

Most temporary child support payments are the result of agreements between separated spouses, not the orders of judges. In either case, the same standards are supposed to be applied to temporary and permanent support awards. The amount of child support accepted temporarily may set a precedent for the later permanent award. The time just after spouses separate is often a period of great emotional vulnerability. They may be reluctant to argue over the amount of child support, but if either one is not satisfied, it is important that she or he take the time at that point to assess needs and review the local standardized child support guidelines before asking for a specific amount. If a mother agrees to temporary support payments that are not what she wanted because she needs the money immediately to survive, she should make clear in a letter to her ex-husband or his lawyer that she accepted that amount under protest and will ask for more as part of the final divorce decree. If spouses cannot agree and need to ask a judge to order temporary support, the mother should indicate to the judge that if he grants less than she needs, she intends to ask for more later.

Before a judge awards temporary child support, he will want to be certain that the basic facts the couple has alleged are accurate. For instance, it must be clear that a marriage actually did occur, that the children for whom support is sought are offspring of that marriage (if it is not clear or acknowledged by the father, the mother will have to prove paternity, as discussed below), and that those children are in need of support while the divorce is going forward. Each of those allegations may be challenged by one of the parents. The father, for example, may tell the court that the mother has enough money to support the children without his help. New York has held that temporary child support cannot be awarded to a woman who is wealthy because such an award must be based on a showing of necessity.[2]

A SETTLEMENT IS PREFERABLE

Because taking a dispute over child support to court is an expensive and usually unpleasant experience, it is better for a divorcing couple to reach an out-of-court settlement. But of course it is foolish for either party to accept an agreement that is not fair simply to avoid arguing before a judge.

An agreement between a husband and wife about the amount of child support will be given substantial weight by a court. Although the judge has a separate responsibility to protect the child's interest, he will usually take an agreement between the mother and father as the best evidence of what is adequate for the child. A husband in Colorado, for example, had agreed to purchase life insurance for the benefit of his children and then refused to carry out his promise. The judge ruled that the agreement was valid and that the husband was legally obliged to buy the insurance.[3] However, in a New York case the court decided that the husband had obtained an unfair advantage in a written separation agreement that required him to make child support payments only if his annual income exceeded $15,000. The judge decided that the husband could not avoid his legal responsibility to support his children through that kind of agreement and invalidated it.[4]

A court's responsibility in making child support decisions is greater than its responsibility in other family disputes, such as awarding alimony. The law places a higher priority on the care and maintenance of children than on the support of former wives. Even if child support is not requested in the papers a mother files, the judge may award support because, as one commentator has said, "the courts can hardly allow a child to go hungry merely because the wife failed to include a demand for child support in her complaint."[5]

Connecticut law *directs* judges who are presented with agreements by the husband and wife that include child support to "inquire into the financial resources and actual needs of the spouses and their respective fitness in order to determine whether the agreement . . . is fair and equitable under all the circumstances."[6]

A Florida divorce court showed how far it would go in asserting its concern for the welfare of the child. Although the child in question, a boy, had been born during the marriage, it was clear that he had no blood relationship to the husband. The husband knew that but had signed an amended birth certificate and an affidavit acknowledging that he was the natural parent. At the same time, the mother of the child had agreed that she would not hold her husband legally responsible for the boy's support. In a later action by the mother for child support, the Florida court ruled that the husband would have to support the child because he had acknowledged paternity and because the most important public interest was in providing for the boy.

ALTHOUGH IT IS USUALLY THE FATHER WHO PAYS CHILD SUPPORT, OTHERS MAY BE HELD LIABLE

Most state statutes direct that responsibility for children after divorce must be shared by the father and mother. Connecticut's statute, for example, says that "the *parents* of a minor child of the marriage shall maintain the child according to their *respective abilities*."[7] When the actual financial statements of both parents are considered, however, it is almost always the father who is ordered to pay because he is usually better able to do so. In recent years, courts have placed part of the financial responsibility for children on the mother because of egalitarian constitutional amendments and laws that have been passed and because more women are earning higher incomes.

A Texas court decreed in a case where the children lived with their father that the mother had an obligation to contribute to their support. The judge went so far as to rule that she was required to reduce her own living expenses to "an absolute minimum" so that she could contribute fairly to her children's care.[8]

The obligation to support children can go beyond the mother and father. Grandparents have been held responsible for the support of their grandchildren where the parents are either absent or unable to provide support. Arizona has an unusual statute which provides that, if the parents of the child are themselves minors, the grandparents may be held liable for the support of their grandchildren. Even stepparents, typically stepfathers, have been held responsible for support of their stepchildren. This obligation arises when the stepparent has lived with the children and previously assumed the responsibility for supporting them.[9]

Even the wealth of the child may be a factor in allocating responsibility for support, although the courts have made it clear that the child should not be forced to support himself unless the parents are absolutely unable to do so. This situation usually arises when a child is the beneficiary of an estate or has an income from a trust fund established by a grandparent. A court in the State of Washington found that a trust fund established by a grandfather for a grandchild's education could not be invaded by the parents for general support of the child. In New York, the courts have held that unless there is a clear showing that parents are unable to support their children, it is not good public policy to permit the assets or income of children to become a factor in setting child support. In one case, a New York judge decided that unless a father could show that he was in need, the court would not compel the children or their trustees even to disclose the children's assets or income.[10]

The Connecticut Appellate Court recently found that a trial judge had abused his discretion when he allowed a father to make child support payments by removing money from custodial accounts he had established before the divorce for the benefit of his two children.[11] The same underlying principle was upheld in a Florida case where a father was told that he would not be excused from paying child support because of the money he paid to his minor daughter for work she did for his business. The court ruled that the child's earnings could not be a factor in diminishing the father's primary obligation to support her.[12]

ALTHOUGH IT IS USUALLY THE MOTHER WHO RECEIVES CHILD SUPPORT, OTHERS MAY ALSO RECEIVE IT

The ultimate beneficiary of child support is the child, but the path to that end is not always direct. The request for child support is normally made as part of a divorce complaint initiated by the mother. Because the children are, by definition, minors, it is also usually the mother who receives the child support award. In some cases, however, the divorce decree requires that child support be paid to a father who has received custody or to a nonparental, noncustodial trustee, such as a grandparent, who is appointed by the

judge for the benefit of a child when the judge decides that the
mother is capable of caring for the child but not capable of managing
money.[13]

If custody of the child has been given to someone other than the
mother, the father is normally ordered to make his support payments
to that custodian.[14] The law is clear that any custodian, parent or
not, receives child support as a fiduciary or trustee for the child, not
in a personal capacity.[15] Wide latitude is typically given for expenditure of that money as long as it benefits the child. One New York
case held that if a court ordered support payments to be made until
the child reached age twenty-one, then those payments should still
be made directly to the child's mother for his benefit even though the
child was over eighteen, the age of majority.[16]

PATERNITY

The first basic step in establishing a child support agreement is
to clarify paternity if it is in doubt. If a man is not obviously and legally the father of a child, he has no obligation to support that child.
Most agreements settling a divorce will dispose of the question of
paternity simply be declaring that the children were "issue of the
marriage between the husband and wife." If, however, there are any
circumstances that make paternity uncertain, the wife should try to
obtain a clear, written acknowledgment of paternity from the father.

Although disputes over paternity *sometimes* occur in divorce proceedings where a father alleges that a child born during the marriage
is not his own, the more common occasion for arguing paternity is
when children are born out of wedlock. There the primary motiva-
tion is the same as it was centuries ago when "bastardy proceedings"
began—to force fathers to support their illegitmate children so that
the community does not have to do so. According to ancient English
common law, an illegitimate child had no right to be supported by
his father but was solely the legal responsibility of his mother. That
changed with the adoption of the Elizabethan Poor Law, which not
only established the first statutory obligation for support but made it

clear that illegitimate children could demand aid from their fathers. The law's purpose was to protect the "parish" from being forced to assume responsibility for all the illegitimates born within it. The basic policy continues today, with much greater consequences for the communal treasury because of the enormous number of illegitimate children. During 1982, 19 percent of all births in America—a total of 715,227 babies—were out of wedlock.[17] Most paternity actions are therefore brought by public agencies at the state or local level as a way of recovering from delinquent fathers part of the millions of tax dollars spent each year for the support of illegitimate children.

When a question of paternity is raised as part of a divorce action, the divorce court has the authority to decide who is the father and to fix a support obligation for the child. In the more common situation, a separate paternity suit is initiated on the child's behalf by the IV-D agency. The court hears the evidence, makes a finding, and adds orders of child support if paternity is proved. In both cases, the rules of evidence are the same. Most of the ancient legal presumptions that guided courts in bastardy or paternity proceedings have lost their significance. Today, paternity proceedings are likely to focus less on who was having sexual intercourse with whom and when than on very sophisticated blood tests that can prove paternity.

For example, a traditional legal presumption was that any child born to a married woman was legitimate. In English legal history, as Homer Clark points out, the presumption "could be rebutted only by proof that the mother's husband was impotent or out of England. In a colorful legal phrase, he had to be proved to be "beyond the four seas."[18]

This strong presumption can now be overcome by the submission of blood tests to prove that the father was in fact not the sire of the child in question, even though the offspring was born during the marriage. The Uniform Parentage Act provides that evidence of another man's paternity is admissible in court only if a blood test shows that he may be the father.

Another legal principle, which became known as Lord Mansfield's rule, was established when an English jurist, Lord Mansfield, held in 1777 that "the law of England is clear, that the declaration of a father or mother cannot be admitted to basterdize an issue born after marriage."[19] This principle still enjoys some lingering vitality in a few states of this country.[20]

The presumption of legitimacy remains alive because of the natural inclination of courts to avoid the creation of illegitimate children. Typical of this thinking is a California case in which a man was ordered to pay for the support of his wife's child in spite of the fact that blood tests proved he was not the father.[21]

The original bastardy proceeding was more criminal than civil and therefore required a higher degree of evidence to prove paternity. Most paternity actions today are civil and therefore require only "a preponderance of the evidence" to establish responsibility in the alleged father.

In the past two decades the Supreme Court has gone far in granting equal rights to illegitimate children. In *Levy v Louisiana*, 391 U.S. 68 (1968), illegitimate children were held to be denied their constitutional rights because they could not obtain a recovery for the wrongful death of their mother. In *Glona v American Guarantee and Liability Insurance Company*, 391 U.S. 73 (1968), a mother was similarly found to be deprived of equality by her inability to recover for the death of her illegitimate child.

Since those two decisions in 1968, the Supreme Court has issued more than twenty rulings that have struck down statutory denials of equality to illegitimate children. In 1973, the Court extended that equality to child support when it held in the case of *Gomez v Perez*, 409 U.S. 535 (1973), that "once a state has established a judicially enforceable right on behalf of children to needed support from their natural fathers there is no constitutionally sufficient justification for denying such an essential to a child simply because its natural father has not married its mother."

A man accused of being the father of a child can, of course, end the conflict over paternity by admitting that he is the father. In many states, only the mother or a public agency can initiate a paternity action. More modern statutes also allow the child and/or the father to seek to clarify their relationship.

A statute of limitations is a period of time after a given event during which a legal action about that event can be started. Most states have established a statute of limitations for paternity actions that is relatively short, reflecting the law's traditional concern about forbidding legal claims in which the evidence has grown stale. For example, Connecticut's Statute of Limitations was three years, which meant that a paternity action could be started only if the child in question had not reached his third birthday. Stimulated by Supreme Court decisions striking down such short statutes of limitations, state legislatures and state courts, including Connecticut's, began to extend them all the way to the age of majority. The theory behind this movement was that, as long as a child is a child, he is entitled to ask support from his father. Then Congress, in its 1984 child support law, required all states to raise their statutes of limitations for paternity actions to 18 years.

Although it is not necessary here to provide a detailed explanation of the science of blood testing, I should point out that blood tests are capable of establishing *nonpaternity* in almost 100 percent of the cases in which the defendant is actually not the father. The most dramatic breakthroughs, however, have occurred in recent years in *positive* identification of fathers through new blood testing procedures, including the human leukocyte antigen (HLA) test. This test was developed to prevent rejection in organ transplants by matching white blood corpuscles.[22] It is expensive, but it can establish a link between a man and his offspring with high probability.

The accuracy of blood tests like the HLA means that in the future the law of paternity will be more a law of science or testing than a law of sexual probabilities or evidentiary questions. Nevertheless, some judges will still have a lingering reluctance to accept blood tests, as is seen in the Michigan case in which a child was born to a woman nine months and ten days after she had separated from her husband. In a subsequent divorce proceeding, the woman asked for support of the child, but the husband denied that he was the father and asked for blood tests of the child, the mother, and himself. The trial judge would not even allow the tests, presumably because he wanted to protect the child's legitimacy; he ordered the alleged father to support the child. His decision was later overruled by the Michigan Appeals Court.[23]

A Pennsylvania case presents a more complicated factual situation. There, a husband and wife had engaged in sexual intercourse at least once during the month of the child's conception. They then separated, and for four years the husband voluntarily paid child support. Later, for other reasons, the mother sought to deny her ex-husband's paternity and asked that he be ordered to have blood tests. The judge refused the request, saying that the parties had acted as if the man was the father and the law should accept that as conclusive.[24]

THE AMOUNT OF CHILD SUPPORT SHOULD MEET THE REAL COSTS OF CHILD REARING

The most important element of child support negotiations is the support itself—how much will be given. We have seen that the establishment of child support awards is the work of individual judges who are guided by generalized standards in state statutes but often reach inconsistent results. We also know that most child support awards are inadequate—they do not cover the actual cost of raising children—because they are too often based on incorrect estimates and because many judges consider the income of the father more than the needs of the child in setting child support. Mothers can remedy those problems by being meticulous and exhaustive in their estimate of what raising a child will cost.

The statutory standard of the state where the divorcing couple lives is a good place to begin the calculations because it establishes overall guidelines. Connecticut's law is typical in directing the judge who will make a child support order to "consider the age, health, station, occupation, earning capacity, amount and sources of income, estate, vocational skills and employability of each of the parents, and the age, health, station, occupation, educational status and expectation, amount and sources of income, vocational skills, employability, estate and needs of the child."[25]

Section 15-E of the Uniform Parentage Act, which has been adopted in 15 states, is simiarly extensive:

> In determining the amount to be paid by a parent for support of the child in the period during which the duty of support is owed, a court enforcing the obligation of support shall consider all relevant facts, including (1) the needs of the child; (2) the standard of living and circumstances of the parents; (3) the relative financial means of the parents; (4) the earning abilities of the parents; (5) the need and capacity of the child for education including higher education; (6) the age of the child; (7) the financial resources and earning ability of the child; (8) the responsibility of the parents for the support of others; (9) the value of services contributed by the custodial parent.

Every state's IV-D agency is required to translate these general principles into a table of child support payments to be used by the court in establishing child support awards. And some courts establish their own guidelines apart from the IV-D standards. These tables usually reflect the cost of living in the state and contain recommended amounts of support per child at varying levels of paternal income. There is no requirement that the court follow these tables, but divorcing parents or their advisers should obtain a copy of the one for their state from the IV-D agency listed in appendix A or from the clerk of the local family or divorce court. It can help them decide whether their calculation of child support needs is roughly accurate. In some states, like Delaware, the guidelines take on added significance because the family court has adopted them as a "rebuttable presumption." This means that unless one of the parties in a particular case can rebut or refute the appropriateness of the tables, they determine the child support award.

The Delaware formula is worth describing in detail because it is one of the most systematic, comprehensive, and sensible approaches to child support awards that I have seen. Developed by Judge

Elwood Melson, Jr., the formula has been in effect in the statewide
Delaware family court since January 1979 and has been altered by
case law and amendments over the years to handle new or unantici-
pated situations.

Three principles form the basis of the Delaware formula:

- Parents are entitled to keep sufficient income to meet their most basic
  needs in order to encourage continued employment.
- Until the basic needs of children are met, parents should not be per-
  mitted to retain any more income than that required to provide the
  bare necessities for their own self-support.
- Where income is sufficient to cover the basic needs of the parents and
  all dependents, children are entitled to share in any additional income
  so that they can benefit from the absent parent's higher standard of
  living.[26]

The application of these principles begins with a determination of
each parent's net income, a figure derived by deducting from gross
income only those withdrawals that are mandatory (such as taxes or
union dues) and those that help the child (such as court-ordered support payments or medical insurance deductions that cover the child).
Next, a self-support exemption is established by determining the absolute minimum amount of money a parent must have to meet his
basic needs such as food, clothing, shelter, medical care, and job-
related transportation. This figure should approximate the poverty
standard of living for one person in Delaware, unrelated to what the
parent may actually earn or spend. The third step is to set the "minimum primary support needs" of the child. This is done by taking
the minimum amount of money required for each parent (the self-
support exemption) as the base figure and presuming that the first
child residing with the parent increases costs by 40 percent of that
amount, the second and third children by 30 percent each, and each
additional child by 20 percent. Added as allowable elements of the
child's primary support needs are child care costs that the mother
must pay so that she can work and any extraordinary medical ex-

penses for the child. The primary support needs of each child are
then allocated to each parent in proportion to the net income they
have left after their self-support exemption is subtracted.

The Delaware formula does not stop there; the family court has
adopted the goal of ensuring that a child's standard of living will
come as close as possible to what he would have had if his parents
had continued to live together. Therefore, if a parent has net income
remaining after taking care of his primary support obligations (including the expenses of a later spouse and children), 15 percent of
that income is added to his child support payments for the first child,
10 percent for the second and third children, and 5 percent for each
additional child. That investment is called a Standard of Living Adjustment (SOLA). In cases where the father is very wealthy or his income comes in uneven spurts, the court has the option of reviewing
the facts each quarter and ordering a supplemental payment to allow
the child to enjoy the standard of living of the more affluent parent.

I urge divorcing spouses or their advisers to apply this formula to
their factual circumstances as a way of determining how much child
support they need. It has the advantages of relative simplicity,
heightened concern for the child's welfare, and deference to the statutory standard that both parents should be responsible for support of
their children. The basic Delaware approach can also be applied to
joint custody or rotating custody situations by adjusting the figures
for the child's primary support needs and SOLA according to the
proportion of time he spends with each parent. It can also be adjusted to recognize long periods of visitation with the father.

In applying its formula, the Delaware family court has developed
a systematic way of dealing with two troublesome complications
that often arise in child support cases: a parent's voluntary unemployment and his remarriage. If the court decides that the parent's
unemployment is voluntary, it will attribute income to him nonetheless, usually on the basis of an estimate of his earning capacity in the
local job market. If a voluntarily unemployed father has remarried or
is living with someone, up to 50 percent of the income of that other
person is attributed to the father in determining his child support ob-

ligation. When either of the parents is working, his or her self-support exemption is lowered if he or she is married to or living with a person who is also working, because there are two incomes available to that household to meet its basic needs. However, as I have said above, the formula subtracts the costs of a spouse or later children from the father's income before the amount he must pay in SOLA is calculated.

Each state definitely has a IV-D agency child support schedule that should be consulted, although it probably will have less influence on the court than a formula that the court itself has adopted.

A few other state approaches have elements that are worth mentioning here. Wisconsin is unique because it bases child support awards on a fixed percentage of the father's *gross* before-tax income, from 17 percent for one child to 34 percent for five or more children. This formula is undoubtedly the easiest to apply, but it does not allow for complicating factors such as joint custody, remarriage, or cohabitation.

The State of Washington has court-adopted guidelines that, like Delaware's, are based on the net income of parents and the number of children but that increase payments for children as they age. Washington also provides that a father cannot be ordered to pay more than 50 percent of his net income in child support and alimony. Idaho sets a minimum of 40 percent of income that the father must retain as an incentive to continue to work.

Judith Cassetty of the University of Texas, an expert on child support, has developed a different formula for the Texas attorney general's office. She begins by subtracting from each parent's income the poverty standard of living for the number of people living in each parent's household to produce a figure she calls "surplus income." The surplus income of the mother is then subtracted from the surplus income of the father, and the result is divided by the number of people in both households to arrive at a per-person share of surplus income. Multiplying that amount by the number of people in the mother's household gives the child support payment due from the father.

A divorcing couple should also run their family's numbers

through the Cassetty formula to see whether it, the Delaware formula, or their state's guidelines produce the best result. The final step is to compare the results of these formulas to the parents' own estimates of what it costs to support their children at their customary standard. Much scholarly research has been done to determine how much it takes to raise children. Although the results have not always coincided, a pattern emerges.

In 1980, the U.S. Department of Agriculture estimated that it cost between $1,570 and $2,845 a year to raise an urban child at an economy level, $2,085 to $3,450 at a low level, and $3,255 to $5,210 at a moderate level. Those figures vary somewhat in different regions of the country and in farm and rural nonfarm areas. On the basis of USDA data, Philip Eden concluded that raising a child costs 23 percent of the household's disposable income for an infant and 29 percent for a 16- to 17-year-old.[27] The USDA itself projects a 40 percent increase in the cost of child rearing from infancy to age 16. All these studies cover minor children and therefore do not include the extraordinary costs of college education.

As part of his work on a pioneering Wisconsin child support experiment, Jacques Van der Gaag of the University of Wisconsin reviewed eleven studies of the cost of raising children and concluded that one child costs 25 percent of household income, a second and third child cost 12.5 percent each, and each additional child costs 6.5 percent.[28]

Several researchers have found that the percentage of total income spent on children decreases as family income increases. For example, Thomas Espenshade reviewed consumer expenditure surveys done by the Bureau of Labor Statistics and found that upper-income households spend about two-thirds as much of their income on their children as do lower-income households.[29]

None of these estimates includes the value of indirect costs, such as maternal child care and homemaking, although Espenshade estimates that the indirect cost of lost opportunities for mothers who are caring for children is often greater than the direct costs of raising children. Some states now require courts to consider indirect child-care costs in setting child support awards. Divorcing parents should also consider them because after a divorce indirect costs often become direct costs if a mother is forced to seek employment and pay for housekeeping and child care. It is important to remember that the indirect costs of child rearing differ from the direct costs in that they decrease as the child grows older and more self-sufficient.

The father's assets, as well as his income, should be considered in setting a desired level of child support payments. Several state statutes require that to be done; some states specifically authorize courts not only to consider assets but also to allocate them as part of a child support award. In Kansas, for example, courts "may set apart such portion of the property of either the husband or the wife, or both of them, as may seem necessary and proper for the support of all of the minor children of the parties, or either of them."[30] Delaware law allows a court to order one parent to leave the family home, even if he owns it, so that his children and wife "might live there and enjoy the family home as an element of support."[31]

No matter which system is chosen to calculate the child support that is desired, the father and mother need accurate income, asset, and cost-of-living figures from each other. If they can exchange those crucial numbers voluntarily, they are fortunate. If they cannot, they will have to decide whether to use estimates in agreeing on temporary support or wait until they get to court, when the judge will order both of them to file full financial affidavits under oath. If either doubts the accuracy of the other's affidavit, they should not hesitate to challenge it, first out of court and then, if necessary, in court, where each is subject to penalties for perjury.

A New York judge who found that a father's evidence of his financial worth and capacity was intended to confuse the court more than educate it decided to base his award of child support solely on the needs of the children rather than on any indicators of the father's economic capacity.[32]

An unusual example of one father's deceit, probably caused by pride, is found in a Florida case where the man filed affidavits showing his net worth to be more than $1 million. The trial court nonetheless awarded child support of only $1,000 a month to the former spouse. The appeals court in Florida said this was a reasonable decision because the husband's financial statements were false; his finances were overstated, and his home, boat, and Rolls Royce were rented.[33]

In other instances, fathers attempt to "bury" money so that it will not be considered in establishing the level of child support. In South Carolina, one father created a trust into which he put his own property and named himself the beneficiary. The court saw through the fiction and valued the man's interest in the trust as an asset that had to be considered in determining how much child support he was to pay.[34]

CHILD SUPPORT AGREEMENTS SHOULD PROTECT AGAINST INCREASES IN THE COST OF CHILD REARING

Every parent knows that the cost of raising children increases with their age. Older children eat more, cost more to clothe, and have recreational expenses that younger children do not have. That burden of rising costs on divorced mothers with custody of their children has been increased by the continuous rise in the general cost of living while their child support awards have remained unchanged.

Philip Eden has shown that a child support award of $500 that was ordered in 1969 had a real value of only $275 in 1979. Because average income increased dramatically in that same time period, the $500, which represented 33 percent of the father's income in 1969, amounted to only 17 percent of his income in 1979.[35] Mothers must protect themselves against such an unfair fiscal squeeze by providing that their child support payments will rise each year based on the increase in the cost of living during the previous year.

Because judges cherish their discretion in setting child support, they have been reluctant to allow or order automatic cost-of-living escalators in their awards. They have argued that spouses should have the right to return to court for a hearing on needs and resources before an increase can occur. Sometimes their arguments have been more circuitous, as in the case where the Nebraska appeals court threw out a lower court decision that child support would be based on the size of the father's annual bonus. Because the bonus varied from year to year, the court reasoned, the child support award would be harder to observe and enforce.

The attitude of judges toward cost-of-living clauses is changing because of the tremendous impact inflation has had on child support awards and the fact that automatic escalator clauses make it less likely that mothers will return to court, thereby reducing court congestion.

The landmark decision in this changing area of law was rendered by the Court of Appeals of Indiana when it considered a judge's order that a father of two pay $1,200 a month in child support to his former spouse and that he also modify that amount annually by the percentage change in the national Consumer Price Index. The father appealed the order, arguing that the automatic increases deprived him of his statutory right to be heard by a judge before a modification in child support could occur. The Indiana appeals court rejected his claim, holding that automatic cost-of-living increases had the positive effect of sustaining the necessary value of the original child support award. The court dealt with the father's objections this way:

> In summary, we approve the court's order prescribing an adjustment in the amount of child support based upon changes in the consumer price index because the provision (1) gives due regard to the actual needs of the child, (2) uses readily available objective information, (3) requires only a simple calculation, (4) results in judicial economy, (5) reduces expenses for attorney fees, (6) in no way infringes upon the right of the custodial parent or the noncustodial parent to petition the court for modification of the decree due to a substantial and continuing change of circumstances.[36]

The appeals court of the State of Washington was also early in upholding a divorce decree that included a different kind of automatic child-support escalator clause. The father was to pay $200 in support each month plus 20 percent of any future net increase in his earned income and 10 percent of any unearned income. He argued that the order was invalid because it did not consider the needs of the children or the ability of the mother to provide additional support. In sustaining the lower court decision, the Washington appeals court said that automatic increase clauses were a reasonable means of dealing with the problem of inflation and an appropriate way to handle an unexpected, substantial change in circumstances. It also stressed a policy factor that will surely be cited more and more often by courts in these cases:

> In fact, the use of escalation clauses seems to be consonant with public demand to reduce the need of people to continually return to court to modify support decrees as well as the present trend of the judicial system to devise acceptable systems of judicial economy.[37]

Some state courts, like Colorado's, have decided that they will not order automatic cost-of-living increases but will approve them if the father and mother agree.[38]

The Delaware family court encourages, but does not require, exspouses to exchange financial information each year and then use it to recalculate the Delaware formula.[39] The State of Washington's guidelines also urge that an automatic annual increase clause be part of every child support award.

There is no consensus on the best formula for automatic escalator clauses, but most rely on one of the standardized, regularly recalculated, readily available norms such as the Consumer Price Index (CPI). Others use either the CPI or the actual increase in the father's income, depending on which is higher.

Remember that a child support award with an automatic escalator can still be appealed to a court. For instance, if the father's income decreases while the cost of living increases, he can ask the court to modify or eliminate the cost-of-living clause because of the change in his own financial circumstances.

ALLOCATING RESPONSIBILITY FOR SPECIFIC ADDITIONAL COSTS SUCH AS COLLEGE EDUCATION

In addition to a general child support award, the circumstances of a particular case may require that the mother ask her ex-husband for additional sums of money to cover extra costs of their children for educational, medical, dental, or recreational programs. These so-called specific awards are important if the child has extraordinary medical, dental, or educational needs. A woman may, for example, want to oblige her ex-husband to pay the costs of treating their child if the child is either physically disabled or will require psychiatric treatment. The cost of orthodontic treatment is another responsibility to be anticipated and specifically covered, as is tuition at a private school if that is probable.

Since the statutory obligation of a father to support his children traditionally ends when they reach the age of majority, the most significant specific costs to cover in a child support agreement will be college and graduate school education. Specific awards, particularly when agreed to in a separation document, are usually upheld by courts, but not without limits. For example, a father in North Carolina who had signed a separation agreement obliging him to pay a substantial part of his children's preparatory school education later changed his mind and claimed that forcing him to do so would violate his constitutional right of equal protection because his wife could afford to contribute and was not doing so. The judge ruled that since the man had voluntarily signed the agreement, his constitutional rights were not violated.[40]

The typical attitude of courts toward specific awards is exemplified in a Nebraska case where the divorce decree included a minimal amount of child support but directed the father to meet the cost of his children's education and vacations. The state's higher court upheld the decision and ordered the trial judge to oversee the case to determine how much money the father was obligated to pay if the parents could not reach an agreement.[41] A Wisconsin court found that a father who was financially able to pay for a summer camp for his children was obliged to do so even though the initial court decision did not specifically include that obligation. A California court held that a divorce decree requiring the father to "pay all reasonable medical and dental expenses of the children as they come due" required him to reimburse his ex-wife for payments she had made for such health costs.[42]

Fathers who try to avoid paying for their children's college education sometimes argue that they had no role in the selection of the college; that tactic has been generally unsuccessful.[43] However, one Mississippi court decided that because a daughter had had no contact with her father for seven years and had no intention of maintaining any relations with him in the future, the father could not be forced to pay for her college education.[44] New York courts have held that if there is a separation agreement requiring a father to pay for his children's college education, it should be enforced even after the children reach the age of majority. In the event there is no such provision in the separation agreement, the general rule must be that a private college education is necessary only if the circumstances in the given case warrant it. A father can be obligated if he has the financial ability to pay and the children have been raised in a setting where a college education would be expected.[45] In one New York case, for example, a judge ordered the father to pay for his daughter's college education because the daughter had a superior academic record, both parents had postgraduate degrees, and the father was able to afford the tuition.[46] In a New Hampshire case, the trial court directed a father to spend $3,000 a year for each child's education because he had an annual income of $50,000, no children with his second wife, and a very liberal retirement pension.[47]

The same principle was extended to graduate education by a Pennsylvania court that ordered a father to pay for his son's law school education because the son had the necessary desire and ability and the father had the money to finance him even though the father's formal legal obligation ended when the child became eighteen. In reaching its decision, the court concluded that the child would have attended law school if his parents had been together.[48]

There is a strong and consistent line of cases in which courts have held that the fact that a child has reached the age of majority does not excuse his father from paying for college, because a higher education can now be considered a necessity of life, like food and clothing. However, the courts in some states, including Connecticut, do not recognize any obligation of a father to pay for college expenses or other expenses for a child after his eighteenth birthday unless there is a written agreement incorporated in the final judgment.[49]

CONSIDERING THE IMPACT OF FEDERAL INCOME TAX LAWS ON CHILD SUPPORT PAYMENTS

It is important for parents to think about taxes when they are agreeing on a divorce settlement, particularly if they are in a position to determine whether they are to give and receive alimony and/or child support. The Internal Revenue Service's rule is that child support payments are not tax deductible by the father but alimony is. Conversely, alimony payments but not child support payments are taxable to the recipient. If a divorced husband and wife have agreed on the amount of money to be transferred, it is to their overall advantage to have the one with the higher income receive the higher deduction and the one with the lower income assume the greater tax liability. This kind of calculation encourages a higher-earning father to give more money to a lower-earning mother so long as most of it is considered alimony and is therefore deductible by him.

The tendency of divorcing couples not to make it clear whether the payments between them are alimony or child support led in 1961 to a historic decision of the Supreme Court in the case of *Commissioner v Lester*.[50] The so-called Lester rule decrees that when a husband gives a payment to his wife that is a combination of alimony and child support, only those amounts that are specifically designated as child support will be considered child support and therefore will not be deductible. The rest of the payments will be considered alimony, which is deductible by the husband. If the father is allowed to make his payments without any definition of what is alimony and what child support, he will be able to deduct the entire amount of the payment as alimony. This arrangement makes sense for the mother only if as a result she receives an amount of support greater than what she would otherwise get.

Divorce lawyers call this concept "fixing," that is, designating the amount of an award that will be counted as child support or alimony. Courts have often been asked to infer fixing in situations where it is not clear. For instance, one couple's divorce agreement included a signed letter that bound the husband to the payment of $7,000 a year for the benefit of the two children. On the basis of that language, the court found that $7,000 of the husband's overall annual payments to the wife were child support and were therefore not deductible by him.[51] In another case the financial agreement between the father and mother was vaguely stated, but there was a clause specifically providing that thirty dollars of the weekly payments were to be used for support of the children. That was held to be a fixing and therefore the thirty dollars was not deductible by the husband.[52]

Determining whether child support payments have been fixed can be even more complicated when there is more than one source for the husband's obligation; there may be a separation agreement and a somewhat different divorce decree, or even conflicting decrees. The question then becomes what is the true source of the father's obligation to make child support payments. In one case a New York state court directed that all the payments being made by the father to the mother were alimony, but a Mexican divorce decree obtained later included a separation agreement signed by both parties that described the father's contributions as child support. The tax court ruled that the father's payments would be considered alimony and therefore deductible because they were made according to the New York decision and actually paid to the mother through a New York Court.[53]

The statutes of some states, including Iowa, New York, and Wisconsin, direct judges to weigh the tax consequences of a child support award for the father and mother before they make the award.

The other important federal tax factor that must be considered is who will receive the dependency exemption for minor children. The Tax Reform Act of 1984 provides that the parent who has custody, typically the mother, receives the exemption unless one of two circumstances occurs:

1. the noncustodial parent has paid at least $600 a year in support of the child, and the divorce order or agreement (executed before 1985 and not modified after 1984) gives him the exemption; or
2. the custodial parent signs a written declaration that he or she will not claim the exemption and the noncustodial parent attaches the declaration to his or her tax return.

The parent who claims the child as a dependent can also take other deductions for the child's expenses, such as medical costs.

A mother negotiating a child support agreement should utilize the dependency exemption as an element of bargaining or self-protection. If she receives an adequate amount of support, she may want to give her ex-husband the dependency exemption. If not, she should explicitly save it for herself in her agreement; it has value.

PROTECTING CHILD SUPPORT FROM BEING ALTERED BY EXTRANEOUS EVENTS

A good child support agreement will guarantee that support payments will continue at the designated level no matter what else happens between a mother and her ex-husband. It will insulate child support from psychological conflict and economic hardship, from the father's voluntary unemployment, remarriage, failure to enjoy appropriate visitation rights, or bankruptcy. The agreement should explicitly declare that the duty to pay child support is separate and primary and is unaffected by either specifically designated events in the father's life, such as remarriage, or particular behaviors by the mother, such as denial of the father's right to visit his children. As we shall see below, these issues have usually been argued in court as part of actions brought by fathers to reduce or eliminate their child support obligations. In general, courts have sided with the mothers and children and have refused to accept these excuses for reducing child support payments. However, there are many cases that reach the opposite conclusion. This means that mothers will make their positions more secure by covering these questions in a negotiated child support agreement rather than leave them undiscussed and open to later litigation.

Father's Unemployment

The Delaware Child Support Formula, discussed above, treats a father's unemployment the way most courts have. If the unemployment is voluntary, the father's capacity for income, not his actual income, will be the basis for setting a child support amount. The key question, of course, is deciding which unemployment is voluntary and which is not.

The statutes of several states, including Connecticut, use the term *earning capacity* as opposed to actual earnings in describing the factors a judge must consider in making a child support award. This traditional principle was upheld in a California case where the father was a board-certified psychiatrist who said he worked only twenty hours a week because he could not find other work that interested him. The court concluded that he was deliberately avoiding work and so based the child support award on his earning capacity, not his actual earnings.[54]

Some courts have reached opposite conclusions. For instance, the Wisconsin Supreme Court reviewed the case of a father who earned only $3,200 a year but was ordered by the trial judge to pay child support of $200 per month on the basis of his earning capacity. The Supreme Court found inadequate the proof that this particular father could have earned more.[55]

Before his divorce, a father who was a lawyer in North Carolina was working fourteen hours a day. Afterward he worked a more normal day. Although his income was only $1,000 a month before taxes, the divorce court judge ordered him to pay child support of $900 a month. The North Carolina Supreme Court reversed the decision, declaring that it was wrong to consider his earlier income as the basis for child support because his decision to stop working fourteen hours a day was not a deliberate suppression of income.[56]

A Texas appeals court ruled that a trial judge had gone too far in directing an unemployed man who had spent fifteen years trying to obtain a Ph.D. degree to pay a higher level of child support. An Oregon court allowed a father to accept a lower-paying but more satisfying job because it found that the burden on him if he remained in his previous employment would be greater than that on his children if he reduced their support.[57]

Although gifts and loans to a father from his parents are not usually included by courts in fixing his child support obligation because they are temporary, a Washington court considered them after concluding that the gifts were enabling the father to keep his income artificially low to reduce his child support award.[58]

In a New York case, a man with an excellent job left both his wife and his position to take up residence with another woman in Canada. He applied for unemployment compensation there. A New York court found that the man was receiving only $95 a week in Canadian unemployment checks but had not made a serious attempt to find a job comparable to the one he had in New York or equal to his abilities. It therefore sustained a substantial child-support award.

A Texas court extended the test of voluntary unemployment from the father to his second wife in a case in which the father argued that he could not support the children of his first marriage because his income was consumed covering the expenses of his second family. The court nonetheless sent the man to jail for contempt because he had not proved that his second wife was unable to work and contribute to the support of his second family.

A father's capacity to earn was the standard applied by a California judge in an unusual case where the father's income was found to fluctuate cyclically because of the nature of his business. The father maintained that a child support award could be based on his earning capacity only if there was proof that he had deliberately reduced his income. But the California Court of Appeals disagreed, upholding the application of an earning capacity test because it was the fairest standard in the circumstances in serving as a means of averaging fluctuating income.[59]

A mother will improve her position and save herself unnecessary time and cost in court if she can convince her ex-husband to include in a divorce agreement language obliging him to continue to work up to his capacity to earn. If she is able to do so, she should try to include explicit standards such as the number of hours per week to be worked by a self-employed or professional father, or a requirement that the father's income must equal an average of the incomes of other people in his field in the local area.

Visitation Rights

Although most state statutes do not accept a mother's refusal to allow a father to visit his children as an excuse for the father to stop or reduce child support payments, judges will often link the two responsibilities in trying to negotiate an agreement between ex-spouses. New York, Ohio, and Oregon have statutes that explicitly authorize judges to consider frustrated visitation rights in setting child support. Unless a woman lives in one of those states, she should try to include a promise in her child support agreement that arguments over visitation rights will not excuse child support delinquency. Both parents must enter a divorce agreement with the sincere intention to carry out all of its terms, but if a misunderstanding occurs or a promise is intentionally broken, child support should continue because the needs of the children must transcend their parents' disputations and hostilities. Society's first objective is to protect the children. A child should not lack support because of a parent's misdeeds.

There is a case from the state of Washington in which a mother moved her child to another state, thereby effectively preventing her former husband from seeing the child. The court found that although visitation rights had been given to the father in the initial divorce decision, the decree itself did not specifically prevent the mother from moving out of the state. The move, therefore, did not justify the father's suspension of child support payments.[60] However, other courts have cited the loss of visitation rights as a reason to reduce or suspend the father's child support obligation, especially if the mother has enough money to support the child. Such courts have concluded that the welfare of the child is protected and the mother should not benefit from her illegal behavior.[61]

The traditional rule was upheld in a Connecticut case where the Supreme Court found that a trial judge erred when he reduced the father's child support obligations because the mother had taken the child out of the state. However, the Connecticut court stated that a court may consider whether circumstances have placed a financial burden on a parent in relation to visitation and whether it is in the best interest of the children to allow a reduction in support to allow for expenditure of funds on visitation.[62]

A Pennsylvania father stopped paying child support when his ex-wife moved their children to Colorado. The Pennsylvania court held that the general rule of the separation of support and visitation rights still applied. But the judge created a small exception; in the extreme case of a mother who secreted her children away, the court would allow the father to stop paying support. In the case before the court, the father had apparently been aware of the mother's plans and not objected.[63] There are several decisions under the Uniform Reciprocal Enforcement of Support Act (URESA) which hold that the only factor that can be considered in a lawsuit filed under the act is the duty of child support; the question of visitation rights is irrevelant. That was the holding in a Florida case where the father had stopped making child support payments because the mother had refused to allow him overnight visitations with his child.[64]

Since the denial of visitation rights by mothers has emerged as a major concern of divorced fathers, cases linking child support with visitation will undoubtedly continue. This paternal pressure may lead to decisions like the one in California where a court held that denial of visitation rights was not sufficient ground for withholding child support because the child's welfare would thereby be injured. However, the court added that it might consider the mother's behavior as reason to transfer custody to the father, regardless of whether he could show that she was unfit or that he was more able to care for the children.[65]

In the same vein, a New Jersey court allowed a father to reduce his support payments because his wife had denied him visitation rights. It concluded that this was the only enforcement mechanism, short of jailing the mother, that would compel her to allow her ex-husband to see his children.[66]

Remarriage

Because most men who divorce will remarry, a mother should try to protect her children's support payments from being reduced as a result of the costs her ex-husband will assume in his next marriage. The best way to do that is explicitly, through an acknowledgment by the father in the divorce agreement that his obligation to the children takes precedence over any new marital or parental obligations he may have. Such a promise would embody the traditional judicial rule that a father's obligation to the children of his earlier marriage is greater because he was aware of them before he remarried. They came first. The father has also been viewed historically as the spouse who left the marriage, abandoned his children, and therefore had a moral obligation to his offspring. With divorce and remarriage so much more common, moral judgments against fathers have receded. The acknowledged economic pressure of supporting two families has also moved more judges to recognize the father's responsibility to his second family. This trend makes it all the more important for a divorcing mother to try to protect the priority of her children's claim for support from their father.

When considering the effect of remarriage, judges rely heavily on the facts of a particular situation as well as on an evaluation of the motives of the people involved. If the court decides that the father is acting in good faith, he is more likely to receive understanding, and so is his second family. The ultimate question is whether remarriage has so changed the reality of the father's life that it requires a change in the level of child support payments that were awarded at the time of the divorce decree.

The Rhode Island Supreme Court has held that a divorced father has a right to remarry and have a new family and that the cost of living for that new family is properly considered by a judge in ruling on a motion to alter the child support award for the former family. In evaluating the financial impact of the adoption by the father of his second wife's children, the court directed the trial judge to determine whether the father was acting "in good faith" or just trying to strengthen his argument for a reduction in support of the other children.[67]

A remarried father in Louisiana also received permission from a judge to reduce support payments to the children of his first marriage even though his income had increased because he had adopted his new wife's child and she had given birth to another child.[68]

In an Idaho case where the father had remarried and a child was born to this second marriage, the court said that the needs of all parties, the husband, both spouses, and the children of the first and second marriages must be considered by a judge ruling on a request for more support by the first wife.[69]

An underlying public policy in these remarriage cases was expressed by a court in the State of Washington when it noted that one of the purposes of the law of divorce is to allow people to be legally capable of remarrying. It is therefore inconsistent, the court said, to punish those who exercise that legal right.[70] Remarriage sometimes engenders attempts by both ex-spouses to change the level of child support. That was the situation in the Louisiana case in which the mother remarried a man of considerable wealth and claimed that her life-style and living expenses were elevated so much as a result that she needed more support from her ex-husband. He in turn asked the court to lower his child support obligation because of the new husband's wealth. The court rejected both requests, finding that the mother's obligation to her children continued as it had been, the father's income remained the same, and the mother's second husband had no legal obligation to support her children.[71]

Father's Bankruptcy

A divorcing mother may want to make clear in her child support agreement that her ex-husband's bankruptcy will not eliminate his child support obligation, although the law already aims to do that. Congress has prevented parents who are responsible for child support from evading their responsibility by declaring bankruptcy. The formal terminology is that support arrears are not dischargeable. They occupy a preferred status among the various claims of creditors against the bankrupt. That is the rule for past-due child support obligations and future obligations. In other words, bankruptcy does not by itself alter the obligation of a bankrupt father to continue the level of child support payments awarded. The only way he can change that obligation is to go back to the divorce court and seek a modification based on his new financial circumstances.

UNILATERAL REDUCTIONS

A mother should protect herself in her child support agreement from unilateral reductions by her ex-husband because of external events. The most common excuses used by fathers for reducing their payments are that they have made voluntary expenditures for their children or have transferred governmental benefits to the children, that one of the children has reached the age of majority or is earning an income, or that the mother has remarried. Each of these events is foreseeable at the time an agreement is signed or a court order is entered. Therefore, except in extreme circumstances, they do not justify lowering child support payments. A child support agreement should make that clear.

Fathers who fall behind in their child support payments sometimes ask that they be given credit for money they spend on their children for gifts or for costs incurred while the children are with them for visits or vacations. Courts have generally been unwilling to allow these credits because they were foreseeable when child support was originally ordered and because of the legal principle that children have a vested interest in their support from the moment it is due. A Florida court, for instance, has held that past-due, unpaid child support is "a vested property right" and cannot be retroactively reduced.[72] An Oregon court turned back a father's request that his overdue child support be reduced, because of the general rule

against retroactive modifications as well as the facts of the particular
case. He had asked to be given credit for child support payments of
$25 per month that he had made to his ex-wife while his child was
institutionalized, but the court found that during that time the mother
had continued to care for the child and had paid the cost of damage
the child had done which caused his institutionalization.[73] Nevertheless, there are cases where a father may be allowed to modify his
future child support payments if his expenditures for his children,
because of the time they spend with him, are so far beyond what was
contemplated that they represent a change in the initial custody
agreement and support award.[74]

Some fathers defend a reduction of their child support payments
because they have transferred governmental benefits to their children
in place of direct support. A judge's reaction to such a unilateral
move is likely to be determined by whether the father could have
foreseen the availability of the benefits and whether he is otherwise
unable to pay. For example, in one Kansas case a father who became totally and permanently disabled directed that his social security payments be made to his ex-wife for the benefit of their minor
children and stopped paying child support. When she sought to enforce his past-due child support obligation, the court gave him full
credit for the social security benefits she was receiving.[75] Similarly,
a judge in Arizona ruled that a father who had been ordered to pay
half of any income he received for the support of his children could
credit toward that amount his old-age benefits, which were paid to
his minor children.[76]

A father in Missouri was allowed to take a credit for social security payments that had been made to his children. But he could do
that only from the time the social security payments began; he was
not excused from any child support payments that had been due before that time.[77]

There are cases, however, that disallow a father's claim for credit
for governmental benefit payments in place of child support primarily because those payments are assigned unilaterally by the father
in violation of an existing court order and without seeking the

court's permission. That was the result in an Oregon case where the court ruled that a father was reasonably entitled to credit for social security payments made to his child but refused to grant it because the original support order had been issued by a judge who knew there was a possibility that such payments might be made to the child.[78]

In cases where the father is ordered, or agrees, to pay a lump-sum unallocated amount for the support of more than one child, he may try to reduce that sum because of a change in the status of one of the children. This usually happens when one of the children reaches the age of majority and the father unilaterally reduces his child support payments to the mother by a proportionate amount. Judges frown upon such alterations without the prior approval of a court. In an Illinois case, a father of four unilaterally reduced his support payments by one-fourth when each of his children reached the age of majority. His ex-wife sued for the amount of those reductions; the Illinois court, finding that only California, Kansas, and Washington allow pro rata reductions, would not tolerate the father helping himself to such a cut.[79]

A man in Indiana had been ordered to pay a lump sum each month for the support of his four children. When two of them married and left the family residence, the father reduced his support payments to his ex-wife. But the court ordered him to pay the full amount until a judge modified the original child support award or all four of the children reached the age of majority or otherwise became emancipated.[80] In an Illinois case, one child died, but the court held that this did not give the father the right to reduce his unallocated support payments for his other children unless a court approved of that reduction.[81]

A father will occasionally lower his support payments because his minor child has begun to earn an income. That tactic is unlikely to meet with judicial approval. In one case in Louisiana, a father cited his child's temporary employment at a fast-food restaurant as a ground for reducing his child support payments. The court rejected the argument.[82] Similarly, a New Hampshire court held that the fact that a minor child had begun working was not sufficient cause to reduce the father's child support payments because the original divorce decree contained no provision to that effect.[83]

Although ex-husbands who are ordered to pay alimony hope for their ex-wife's remarriage so that they can reduce or stop their payments, some fathers also use their ex-wife's remarriage as an excuse for unilaterally lowering child support payments. A former wife's remarriage and her new husband's wealth are factors that some courts will consider, but they are almost never a justification for unilaterally lowering child support payments.

PROTECTING CHILDREN IN THE EVENT OF THEIR FATHER'S DEATH

A good child support agreement will protect children if their father dies while they are minors by requiring that support payments continue unless there is acceptable, alternative protection for the children such as life insurance or a specific bequest in the father's will.

If a father is behind in his child support payments at the time of his death, that indebtedness can be presented as a claim against his estate and will almost definitely be recognized as legitimate. But what of future child support payments? While the traditional rule was that a father's death terminated his obligation to pay child support, the modern trend of decisions finds a postmortem obligation based either on the specific terminology of a divorce agreement or on the overriding concern the law has for the welfare of children. If the father's estate is the entity other than the government most able to continue care of the children, judges are likely to impose that obligation.

Statutes of some states are already recognizing the change and enforcing the father's postmortem obligation as a matter of law. The Uniform Marriage and Divorce Act says that if a father who was obligated to pay child support dies, "the amount of support may be modified, removed, or commuted to a lump sum payment to the extent just and appropriate to the circumstances, unless there is some contrary provision in the divorce decree or a voluntary agreement between the parties.[84]

When the state has an interest in avoiding financial responsibility for a child born outside a marriage, there is even greater willingness to continue the obligation of the father. Idaho, for example, has a statute that allows a judicially approved child support settlement to be enforced as a claim against the father's estate "in an amount to be determined by the probate court not greater than is provided by the order of settlement, having regard to the age of the child, the ability of the surviving parent to support and educate it, the amount of property left by the deceased parent, and the number, age, and financial condition of those other persons legally entitled to support by the deceased parent during his or her lifetime."[85]

The strongest and most common argument against a father's postmortem responsibility is that children of divorce are thereby granted rights greater than those enjoyed by children of married families, whose parents are legally able to disinherit them in a will. Some have argued that ordering a father's estate to continue to make child support payments denies the basic legal principle that an individual is free to dispose of his estate as he wishes. But the Idaho Supreme Court expressed the contrary argument for continuing the father's child support obligation after death when it wrote:

> When parents obtain a divorce and one parent takes custody of the children, the likelihood of an embittered or disinterested parent disinheriting a child in the other spouse's custody increases.[86]

An Illinois statute that provided for continued support after death for children of divorced parents was challenged as a denial of equal protection for children of married families. However the Supreme Court of Illinois upheld the statute, declaring that the child of a married parent has some "indirect security against the possible loss of support due to disinheritance" because the remaining parent is protected by the law from being totally disinherited. The court added:

While it is comparatively rare for a nondivorced parent to leave a spouse and their children out of a will, it is not so uncommon for a divorced parent to do so. . . . A divorced parent may establish a new family which may command primary allegiance in the subsequent will. The well-being of children of a former marriage may seem more remote to a noncustodial parent than the well-being of those children over whom that same parent has immediate care and custody. In addition, the divorced parent may harbor animosity toward a former spouse, which disposition might obscure the natural tendency to provide in a will for their mutual children.[87]

Courts attach great importance to the specific wording of a child support agreement or order in deciding whether a father's estate is obligated to support his children, as can be seen in the following three cases.

A New Mexico court found that because a father had been ordered to make child support payments until his child reached the age of majority, the minor child was entitled to collect those payments from the father's estate.[88] A New York court strictly interpreted a support agreement when it declared that a minor child could not collect support from his deceased father's estate because the original child support agreement did not include a fixed obligation for a fixed period of time, even though the agreement contained words that said that it inured "to the benefit of and [was] binding upon the parties . . ., the heirs, personal representatives, administrators, and assigns."[89] In a Michigan case, an infant was declared to have a claim against his father's estate because the divorce decree bound the father to make a specific monthly support payment "until the further order of the court."[90]

While parties to a divorce, and courts that preside over divorces, are increasingly ordering fathers to maintain life insurance as security for children's support, it has also been held by the Mississippi high court that an order to maintain life insurance is proof that ordinary child support payments are meant to stop if the father dies.[91] A father's agreement to provide life insurance for the benefit of his children cannot go beyond either the child's minority or a time when the father would be expected to continue to support his child for some special reason, such as a disability or the need for a college education. The order to maintain life insurance is seen as a way of providing security for the continued upholding by the father of his legal obligation.[92] It is comparable to an order directing a father to establish a trust fund to benefit his children, which can be in force only so long as the child is either a minor or entitled to some special support during the beginning of his majority.[93]

A father's obligation may be reduced or eliminated if, in his will, he makes a bequest to his children and indicates that it is intended to take the place of child support. This result is particularly likely if the bequest is of greater value than the child support obligation. If not, a ruling like the one issued by the appeals court in Oklahoma is possible. It found no clear showing that the father's bequest to his children was intended to take the place of child support, and the value of that bequest was uncertain. Therefore the court would not deny the children's claim for support from their father's estate. A Wyoming court even ruled that a father's estate must receive credit for money paid for the benefit of the children as a family allowance during the time the estate was being probated.[94]

The message of these cases for mothers is clear. Their support agreements must contain either a pledge that their ex-husband's estate will continue to support their children at the agreed amount, or that he will maintain a specific value of life insurance to benefit the children, or that he will make specific bequests to the children in his will that will be of a value equal to or greater than his child support obligation. The mother should receive proof that the father has carried out these promises.

CLARIFYING HOW LONG YOUR CHILD SUPPORT AGREEMENT WILL LAST

Child support should be paid as long as the child is a child, that is, until he or she reaches the age of 18. That obvious premise should be stated in the agreement to protect the mother from some unforeseen event, such as her child's temporary departure from high school and acceptance of a job, which might give her ex-husband cause to consider terminating support. It is also important to state the specific circumstances in which support will continue after the age of majority. The cost of higher education, which I have already discussed, is the most common continuing obligation. The description of this obligation should be left as open-ended as possible in case the child goes on to graduate school. It is also important to provide for continuing support if the child is unable to support himself after he reaches the age of majority because he is physically or psychologically disabled.

Courts have generally recognized that a father's support obligation remains in force after the age of majority in these special circumstances, but mothers can save themselves the cost and time of litigation by clarifying the obligation in their support agreement or court-ordered award.

Although most courts today view higher education as a necessity, there are decisions relieving a father of this obligation, particularly when it appears that the child is effectively emancipated. Such a judgment was the basis of a Texas appeals court ruling which held that a child who had begun a six-year premedical degree program in a city far from either parent had thereby declared himself emancipated and was no longer entitled to child support from his father.[95]

There are very few exceptions to the rule that a parent has an obligation toward a disabled child that continues after the majority age. However, one example is the Pennsylvania case where the father was held not liable to support his eighteen-year-old son or to pay for his psychiatric care because the parents had signed an agreement that support would end when the boy reached his majority, and there was no evidence that the son was unable to find employment and support himself.[96]

The more common rule was expressed in a Utah case in which a father was ordered to continue paying support for his retarded and incompetent daughter even though she no longer satisfied the statutory definition of a "child."[97]

Another ground for termination of child support payments is the minor child's marriage. Most courts view a child's marriage as self-emancipation. This theory was adopted by an Arizona court in a case where the divorce decree said that the father's child support obligation continued "until majority or further order of the court." When the daughter married, the father was found to be no longer liable for support payments even though he did not immediately return to the court to modify his obligation. The court concluded that the daughter's marriage was the legal equivalent of reaching the age of majority.[98]

A Tennessee appeals court reached the same conclusion and ordered a creative remedy in a case where a father had continued to pay child support to his former wife even after their minor daughter married. When the father complained to a court, it held that the mother had "improperly received" $2,450. The court directed that she be given credit for $700 toward the expense of her daughter's wedding but that the rest of the overpayment be subtracted from future alimony.[99]

An extraordinary capsulized comment on the state of marriage and responsibility in our time is the Missouri decision in which a judge concluded that a minor daughter was not entitled to child support from her father after she had been married, even though she was later divorced while *still a minor*.[100]

OBTAINING SECURITY FOR SUPPORT

Because statistics show that fewer than half the divorced mothers in America receive the child support that they are owed, a woman must include terms in her support agreement that will raise the probability of her ex-husband's payments. This could be the most important part of the agreement because, without security, the agreement may amount to no more than a promise that is easily broken. There are many possible forms of preventive security. A woman can require her husband to post a bond to guarantee his adherence, just as a private contractor is often required to buy a bond in the name of his client to guarantee his performance. If her ex-husband's child support payments stop, the bond is called and takes his place in fulfilling the support obligation. It is essentially a form of insurance. A lien against property owned by the ex-husband can be used in the same way. If he defaults in payments, the lien is activated and the property is liquidated to support the children. This is like the lien a bank places on property that is bought with mortgage money obtained from the bank.

Although it is difficult to buy insurance to guarantee performance of a voluntary obligation such as child support, a woman may want to ask her husband to maintain life insurance for the benefit of their children so that they will be protected from his death if not from his failure to pay support during his life.

If the father is wealthy at the time of his divorce but the mother doubts his long-term financial stability or interest in her children, she may want to ask that he establish a trust fund, with her or some third person as the trustee, that will actually make the child support payments. Judges sometimes use this device if they doubt a father's responsibility. A trustee is appointed by the court to preserve the assets of the fund and to make them available to the children as needed. The trustee must report periodically to the court.

Many state child support statutes, including Connecticut's, give judges the authority to "direct security to be given" for child support. That authority has increasingly been used preventively to guarantee child support payments by requiring a father to assign part of his wages or income for child support. As we shall see in chapters 5 and 6, which discuss enforcement of child support orders, income assignments that begin with the original child support order or go into effect automatically if a father is more than thirty days in default are the best way to secure child support payments.

A mother who is negotiating a child support agreement with her ex-husband will optimize her children's position if their father will agree in writing to assign part of his income weekly or monthly to support his children. The assignment can then be sent as an order to the sources of the ex-husband's income, such as his employer, bank, or trustee, who will automatically deduct the child support payments from the money he is otherwise owed and pay them to the mother.

CHAPTER FOUR

How to Change
a Child Support Award

INTRODUCTION

If a divorcing couple follows the prescriptions offered in the preceding chapter, they do not have to worry about returning to court to change their child support award. They have agreed to an adequate award that will self-adjust over time to meet increased costs. The mother has been granted additional sums to cover specific costs, such as her children's college expenses. Her agreement protects her from suffering as a result of extraneous events, including her ex-husband's remarriage, voluntary unemployment, or even his death. Perhaps, a sudden involuntary drop in his income will enable the father to go back to the judge to ask that his child support obligation be reduced, and the mother will have to return to defend against that. But otherwise she has emerged from her child support negotiations with an agreement that will make it very unlikely she will have to call on courts to resolve a dispute with her ex-husband.

But this happy result will not be achieved by everyone. Some divorced couples will need to return to their lawyer and the court. There are two reasons why people usually try to change support awards—either the mother wants to get more, or the father wants to give less. Like the previous chapter, this one will focus on helping mothers maintain or increase the amount of support they are currently receiving.

PROCEDURES

Child support awards are always modifiable because court files in divorce cases always remain open. The court retains jurisdiction of a divorce case after the decree is issued; therefore, an attempt to increase child support payments does not require the initiation of a new lawsuit. A lawyer simply files a "motion to modify" as part of the earlier case no matter how much time has passed since the divorce. That is true even if the divorced couple signed a separate child support agreement that was not part of the court's divorce decree. The legal system always preserves the right to make certain that children are being adequately supported, regardless of what the parents may have decided.

For example, a father and mother in New Jersey signed a separation agreement which provided that it could be modified only by consent of both parties; that agreement was incorporated into their divorce decree. When the father asked that his support payments be reduced because his ex-wife, who had a professional degree, was avoiding work, she objected, citing their prior agreement requiring her consent to any changes. But the New Jersey Supreme Court held that the agreement could not be used to prohibit the court from asking whether circumstances had changed enough to merit a change in support.[1]

In a similar case, the Vermont Supreme Court declared that an agreement between parents about child support could not be interpreted as just another contract because it affected the interests of children. Therefore, the court had the ability to modify the parents' agreement if circumstances changed.[2]

It is vital to understand the limits of what a mother can accomplish with a motion to increase child support. She cannot use it to get a judge to hold another hearing on the same facts that were the basis of her original support order. If she is unhappy with the original decision and the facts have not changed, all she can do is go to a higher court and allege that the decision was based on legal errors or was totally unsupported by the facts. The trial court that heard the case in the first place will hear it again and increase support payments only if it can be shown that the financial needs or capacities of the mother, father, or children have changed substantially in a way that was unforeseen and probably will be permanent. If it can be proved to the court that important facts were not known by one of the parties and the court at the original hearing, the judge may also agree to hear the case again.

PROVING CHANGED CIRCUMSTANCES

Every state's child support laws allow for modification of child support orders only if circumstances have changed, but the states vary somewhat on how they define the amount of change required. The Uniform Marriage and Divorce Act is most demanding in that it allows a modification of the original award "only upon a showing of changed circumstances so substantial and continuing as to make the terms unconscionable."[3] Although the drafters of this law have explained that their purpose in choosing this language was "to discourage repeated or insubstantial motions for modification," only two states—Colorado and Montana—have adopted it. Indiana and Missouri also enacted the uniform language but changed the word *unconscionable* to the softer *unreasonable.* Connecticut's law says simply that a child support award can be changed "upon a showing of a substantial change in the circumstances of either party."[4] That language is typical of what is found in most states.

In deciding whether to modify a child support award, a judge will normally consider the same factors that were considered by the court that first issued the order. The legal burden will be on the moving party—usually the mother—to prove her case, not on her ex-husband to disprove it. The mother will not be able to ask for an increase in support payments that were made before the date on which she filed her motion for modification, just as her ex-husband will not be able to ask for a reduction in payments that he should have paid before the date on which he filed his motion for modification. Men who are delinquent in child support payments often try to convince a judge to order a retroactive reduction of the support amount as a way to reduce that indebtedess, but, unless the law in the state permits retroactive modification of support orders, they should fail.

MOTHERS' MOTIONS FOR MORE

Some state courts have said that they will increase a child support award only if the evidence shows that the needs of the children have increased *and* that the father's ability to pay has gone up enough, in relation to their needs and the mother's income, to enable him to give more.[5] Other courts have simply required that the evidence show that the father's income has increased, regardless of whether the children's needs have also increased. Those courts aim to provide the children with a level of support comparable to what they could have enjoyed if their family had remained intact.[6]

As a general rule, if a mother is asking for more support for her children, she should be ready to prove that her ex-husband can afford it or, at least, is better able to meet a rise in costs than she is. To do so, she needs to know what his income and assets are. This information can be obtained through negotiations with him or his lawyer. If the attempt fails, she should proceed to file her request for more money with the court anyway on the assumption that her ex-husband *can* afford it. Once in court, he will have to file a personal financial statement under oath.

What kinds of change in children's circumstances justify an increase in support? The answer to this question reads like the list of the events that I advise divorcing couples to anticipate and provide for in their child support agreement (see chap. 3)—the increasing costs that come naturally as children age, the general increase in the cost of living that inevitably affects the cost of raising children, and special expenses such as college tuition and uncovered medical or psychiatric care.

In a 1980 decision, a Florida court found that while inflation had kept a father's purchasing power stable even though his income had increased, it had substantially decreased the mother's purchasing power. In the meantime, the mother's costs had increased because the children had reached adolescence. The court ordered the father to increase his support payments.[7]

An Arizona court held that a general increase in the cost of raising children since a divorce had been granted was enough of a change to justify an increase in child support from the father, particularly because his income has also increased.[8]

The increasing cost of raising a child as the child grows older led a Missouri court to order the father to give more support to his ex-wife for their child. The court was also impressed by the fact that the father's income had gone up and his second wife was employed.[9]

A Wisconsin judge decided that evidence proving a 40 percent increase in the cost of living since the original child support order was an acceptable basis for a proportionate increase in the award.[10]

One New Jersey judge went further and held that it was not even necessary to submit proof that the cost of living had gone up since the original support order. The increase was simply acknowledged as a fact by the judge.[11]

But the Maine Supreme Court, in a 1981 decision, cautioned against increasing child support because of inflation. Citing inflation, a mother who received $250 a month in child support asked for more four years after the initial award. The court said she had to prove that inflation had increased her costs of child rearing. Since she had not done so, her support remained unchanged.[12]

A mother in Illinois requested and received an increase in support even though her ex-husband proved that she had gone to work and earned an income since the divorce. The court found that his income had also increased, the cost of the children's clothing had doubled, the wife's entertainment expenses had tripled because she and the children went out for dinner more often, and she had hired a full-time babysitter so that she could work.[13]

Apart from general increases in the cost of living and raising children, the most common reason for trying to modify child support awards is to compel fathers to pay educational expenses. As I said in chapter 3, some courts today are very likely to view college education as a necessity and to order a father to meet all or part of its costs, even if his child has passed the legal age of majority, when the parent's obligation is supposed to end. Typical of this conclusion is a Missouri case in which the court acknowledged that a valid separation agreement entered by the mother and father provided for support to end when the child became eighteen years old but nonetheless ordered the man to increase his payments because his child had begun college. Here again the judge was encouraged by evidence showing that the father's income had grown.[14] However, in Connecticut the Supreme Court has held that a father has no obligation to support a child after his eighteenth birthday unless there is an agreement providing for support or payment of college expenses.[15]

A New Mexico court also ordered a father to increase support payments because two of his children were in a private school and a third, his youngest, was about to enter. The court noted that the father's annual income had risen from $42,000 to $87,000.[16] Another example of special factors justifying a change in child support is the Oregon case where a father was assessed for his children's medical and dental expenses that were not covered by his health insurance.[17]

These cases demonstrate that a mother's ability to prove that her ex-husband is financially able is critical to her ability to obtain more support for her children. For example, the appeals court in North Dakota reversed a trial court decision that a father was unable to pay child support because it found evidence that his monthly income exceded his expenses and he had just bought a new automobile.[18]

According to a Maine case, the assets and income of the mother were not even relevant in an action to increase child support if the husband's resources were shown to be adequate to meet those higher costs.[19] A Michigan court raised a man's child support obligation because his children's costs had increased when they became teenagers and his resources had gone up as a result of his promotion from third mate to captain of a vessel, even though he showed that his promotion might not be permanent.[20]

The income of a father's second wife is also relevant to his ability to pay. In 1983, the Montana Supreme Court allowed a mother to obtain information about the bank account and business clients of her ex-husband's new wife as part of an action to increase his child support obligation.[21]

FATHERS' MOTIONS FOR LESS

In chapter 3, I discussed several of the specific reasons why fathers commonly seek to lower their child support and how courts have generally responded to those attempts. I will not repeat that discussion here. In general terms, the arguments usually presented for reducing support are as follows: (1) the father's unemployment or job change; (2) the mother's denial of visitation rights to the father; (3) the father's remarriage; (4) the father's bankruptcy; (5) the father's voluntary expenditures for the children beyond the child support order; (6) the father's transfer of governmental benefits to the children; (7) the fact that one of the children has reached the age of majority or has been otherwise emancipated; (8) the fact that the child has an income; and (9) the mother's remarriage. For a full discussion of these arguments for reducing a father's obligation, see chapter 3.

The argument most often cited by fathers for reducing their child support obligations is a drop in their ability to pay. In evaluating that claim, a court will first determine whether the father's income has really declined and then whether he could have avoided that decrease. Finally, the judge will decide whether the father's reduction in income is substantial enough, in relation to his children's needs and his ex-wife's resources, to justify a reduction in his child support obligation. The case law suggests that a father will have to make a very strong argument to receive a court's permission to lower his support of his children. This burden of proof on the father is entirely appropriate because of the factual evidence which shows that mothers rarely receive in support what it actually costs them to care for their children.

In a Florida case, a father who had been ordered to pay $75 a week in child support was out of work because of a strike that caused his annual income to drop from $18,000 to $12,000. The father's move for a reduction in support payments to $60 weekly was granted by the trial court. But the appeals court reversed, saying that the needs of the children had not changed and that the father's loss of income because of the strike was temporary.[22]

A father in Alaska asked that his $400 monthly support obligation be cut because his income had dropped by $400 per month and his expenses were now $300 greater than his income. The court refused to cut his obligation because it found that the mother's resources were very limited and that the father still had a $1,000 monthly income available to him. His personal expenses had to be reduced before his child support payments.[23]

However, judges will allow fathers to reduce their support payments if the facts clearly justify it. Such was certainly the result in the Louisiana case where a man was unemployed and had no assets other than $1,500 in jewelry, the corporation of which he had been president was in bankruptcy, and his personal liabilities equaled almost one million dollars. The court allowed this father to reduce his monthly child support payment from $2,500 to $100.[24]

A father's disability will usually justify a reduction in his child support obligation. For example, an Illinois court ordered a cut in support after the evidence demonstrated that the father had become disabled and therefore unemployed and the mother's earned income had increased.[25]

After accepting the principle that in cases where hardship is inevitable the brunt of sacrifice for child support should be placed on the father, a Texas appeals court nonetheless found that in the case before it a father's child support obligation should be reduced. Seven days after his divorce he was hospitalized with leukemia and a ruptured spleen, which substantially raised his necessary expenses.[26]

In cases where there has been an unavoidable decline in a father's income, courts are more willing to grant a reduction in his support obligation if the mother is employed or could reasonably be expected to be employed. Thus, when a mother in Maine obtained a job, her former husband asked the court to reduce his weekly child support payments from $75 to $50. The Supreme Court upheld the reduction, declaring that each parent must participate in the support of a child in proportion to his or her ability to pay.[27]

A Michigan appeals court decided that a lower court erred when it increased a father's child support obligation because his ex-wife had left her job to become a student, even though her education would eventually enable her to earn a higher income.[28]

A final example of judges' willingness to apply principles of law equally to fathers and mothers in child support matters is the Texas case in which the appeals court affirmed that it was proper for the trial court to consider the income of the mother's new husband because, although he had no legal obligation to support her children, *his* capacity to support *her* would determine how much money she had left to care for the children.[29]

CHAPTER FIVE

How to Collect Child Support from a Delinquent Father

Like the last chapter on modifying child support orders, this one on enforcing those orders would be unnecessary if a divorced couple had a good child support agreement. For example, the mother would already have provided for automatic assignments of her ex-husband's income to meet his child support obligation, and if his income failed, she would have had preventive security in place —an attachment on his property or a bond to assume his obligation. But enforcement is the most active area of child support law because many fathers are not paying and many mothers are not adequately protecting themselves from that eventuality. In the summer of 1984, Congress and the president agreed on significant changes in American child support law when they adopted the Child Support Enforcement Amendments of 1984, Public Law 98-378 (hereinafter called the 1984 Act), which went into effect on October 1, 1985. Each state is required to bring its laws up to minimum federal standards, which will substantially improve a mother's chances of collecting from her ex-husband.

In this chapter, I will explain what can be done if a father stops paying child support. Because of the 1984 Act, the legal weapons available to mothers now are much greater than they were a few years ago. For too long, too many fathers have been allowed to ignore their children and assume that the legal system would neither pursue nor punish them. That will no longer be a safe assumption.

If our experience in Connecticut is a guide, private attorneys will not immediately be aware of, or utilize, the new enforcement procedures of the 1984 Act. Therefore, mothers should learn them so they can press their lawyers to use them.

Like a motion to modify a child support order, a motion to enforce it is brought as part of the original divorce judgment or child support decree, not as a totally new lawsuit.

If the children are receiving welfare payments, the mother has assigned their legal right to be supported by their father to the state. Her ex-husband should therefore have been making his payments to the state; if he has not, attorneys for the state will try to enforce the order and collect the support. The 1984 Act gives mothers a vested interest in that effort for the first time because it provides that they can keep the first $50 of child support collected each month without losing any of their welfare payments. Mothers will also receive a report at least once each year on how much support has been collected from their ex-husband. The federal government clearly hopes that this information will encourage women to leave the welfare rolls and find jobs because they will be able to estimate what their earned income plus anticipated support payments might be.

If a mother is not a welfare recipient, the state collection services available to her are even more substantially improved by the 1984 Act. Since 1974, as we have seen, state child support agencies have been required to assist non-AFDC recipients because of the decision of Congress that it makes sense to spend some public money to help women collect child support because they would otherwise find their way to the welfare rolls, where they would exact much more from the public treasury. In fact, however, many states have emphasized AFDC collections, perhaps because all the money raised thereby went to state and federal governments. Non-AFDC cases were often delayed or never brought at all.

The 1984 Act seeks to rectify this discrepancy by equalizing the direct federal fiscal incentives for AFDC and non-AFDC cases and by making all the mandatory collection tools of the act (for example, income assignments and federal tax intercepts) available to nonwelfare cases for the first time. The states may charge a non-AFDC mother an application fee of no more than $25 plus the *actual* costs of collection, although the delinquent father is more likely to be asked to pick up the costs of collection. For many women not poor enough to qualify for welfare but not rich enough to afford a lawyer, the right to be represented by a public attorney will be the path to economic stability. A mother can contact a support enforcement lawyer by calling her state's support agency, listed in appendix A.

HOW LONG CAN A WOMAN WAIT?

If a woman waits too long to initiate an enforcement action for child support or passively accepts reduction of her ex-husband's payments, she may be prevented from ever collecting the money she is owed. Some states have a statute of limitations for child support enforcement, that is, a period of time during which the enforcement action must be started. In states where there is no statute of limitations, another traditional legal doctrine, known as *laches*, may be used as a defense by a delinquent father. *Laches* means acquiescence to a condition over so long a period of time that you are prevented from beginning a legal action on the basis of that condition. The doctrine of laches was applied in a Florida case where a court held that a divorced mother could not successfully prosecute her ex-husband for child support he owed her because she had accepted lower payments for several years.[1] Similarily, in an Ohio case a woman was denied back child-support payments because for ten years she had lived according to an understanding with her ex-husband that bound her not to demand child support from him if he did not visit the child.[2]

The defense of laches will not be successful if a judge determines either that the father did not suffer as a result of his ex-wife's delay in asserting her claim or that the child's need for adequate support is simply of greater concern than the fact that the mother waited so long. Courts are less likely to allow the father's defense of laches in an action to garnish his wages or attach his property than in a contempt action that might result in his incarceration.[3]

FIRST, TRY PERSUASION

In child support, as in other matters of conflict, going to court should be the last resort. Unless a woman fears that her ex-husband will injure her physically, she should notify him that she intends to consult a lawyer by a certain date if he fails to pay the child support he owes her. If he remains delinquent, as is probable, she should immediately contact her private attorney or child support agency. This representative, in turn, should try to pressure the ex-husband into voluntary payment by sending bills, initiating telephone reminders, and threatening contempt-of-court proceedings. If he remains unresponsive, it is time to go to court.

CONTEMPT

A child support award is an order by a judge that a person must do something. As with any other judicial order, if the person ignores or violates the award, he can be held in contempt of court and suffer various forms of punishment, including a jail sentence in appropriate circumstances. Nonsupport is also a criminal offense in most states, and a conviction can result in a jail sentence. However, bringing a criminal action is often avoided because the process must be started by a prosecutor, who is normally busy with other criminal matters, whereas civil contempt proceedings are initiated by the mother's attorney, whether he is private or public. Criminal proceedings for nonsupport, like all other criminal prosecutions, require a higher standard of proof, particularly on the question of whether the father's failure to pay child support was willful. Nevertheless, in the most flagrant cases, the prosecuting authorities may wish to make an example of a father who has neglected his children by seeking a conviction.

In most cases of unpaid child support, going to court to hold a father in contempt and thereby threaten him with jail is enough to move him to action. He will either pay his overdue obligation or consent to some court-supervised remedy, such as a withholding from his income or an attachment on his property.

However, there remain cases in which a contempt order will have to be pursued either as punishment for truly irresponsible past behavior or, more likely, as an inducement to present and future good behavior. In those cases a civil contempt order will be imposed on a delinquent father who the court believes is able to pay child support. He will be jailed until he does pay.

Although judges throughout America have been reluctant to use their contempt powers to jail men in child support cases, studies done in Michigan by David Chambers show that such orders and jailings have had a dramatically positive effect on child support payments. This certainly seems logical. I will discuss Chambers' recommendations for public policy in the next chapter (6).

To hold a father in contempt of his support order, a court must conclude that (1) he was able to pay, (2) he knew about the order, and (3) he intentionally refused to make payments without any good explanation. The requirement that the father must be able to pay before he can be found guilty of contempt of court is the reason this procedure does not violate the constitutional prohibition against imprisoning people solely because they are in debt. In fighting a contempt proceeding, a father can use the same arguments he might use against his ex-wife's attempt to increase child support or in his own attempt to reduce or terminate his obligation (discussed in chaps. 3 and 4).

The father is most likely to defend himself by trying to prove that he was unable to pay and therefore is not guilty of willfully violating the judge's orders. He will have to show that his inability to pay is not the result of his own act. Here again the trial judge must make a subjective conclusion about the father's circumstances and his sincerity. In an Indiana case, for instance, a father defended himself against a contempt charge by pointing to his remarriage and the additional financial responsibilities it entailed. The court nonetheless held him in contempt because it found that his income was sufficient to continue child support and that he had simply diverted that money to his new family.[4]

The Texas courts have been very demanding in evaluating fathers' claims of poverty. A father in Texas must demonstrate not only that he is insolvent through no fault of his own but also that he lacked any assets which could be mortgaged or sold to raise the money he owed his children and that he had tried and failed to borrow the money. Only if the court accepts his proof on all those points will the father avoid being held in contempt.[5] One Texas judge would not accept a man's argument that he was unable to pay child support of $150 a month, because the judge found that the father was making car payments of $140 per month, had remarried, and was successfully supporting his new family.[6]

There are other contempt cases in which a father has defended himself not on the basis of inability but of misunderstanding, usually a mistaken belief that he was not obligated, for some external reason, to pay child support. In one Alabama case, for instance, a father defended against a contempt charge by saying that he believed that his child's maternal grandparents were supporting the child and therefore he was no longer obligated to do so because there was no need. The court rejected that argument.[7] The same result greeted a father's contention that he was not in contempt because his child was earning money. The judge found that it was the father's failure to support his child that had forced the boy to take a job.

Other defenses to a contempt claim that are asserted by fathers have a familiar ring: (1) although he had not obeyed the court's support order, the father had made other payments for the benefit of the children, particularly if they were in his custody for part of the time; (2) the mother had breached the underlying agreement by refusing to allow her ex-husband to enjoy his court-ordered visitation rights; and (3) the mother had agreed out of court that the father could reduce or stop his child support payments.

The law is clear that none of these claims is an adequate defense because each of them involves unilateral action by the father, unapproved by the court that issued the award. In practice, however, judges will sometimes consider these circumstances (especially indirect compliance by the father and denial of visitation rights by the mother) in deciding whether to hold the father in contempt or to negotiate an agreement.

The following are examples of cases in which these defenses have saved a father from contempt:

- A father in Florida was voluntarily paying the college tuitions and living expenses of his children, which amounted to a sum greater than his child support obligation. The Florida court allowed the father to claim those payments as credit and to assert them as a defense to a contempt charge.[8]
- Although the giving of gifts, monetary or other, by a father to his children will rarely be allowed as credit for past-due child support, in one Maryland case the father had given checks to the children, who endorsed them and gave them to their mother. She used the money for the children's care. The court felt that this father was entitled to credit.[9]
- In an Alabama case, a mother sent her child to live with his father for more than a year because she was emotionally and physically disabled. Later, the mother tried to hold the father in contempt for his failure to pay child support to her during the time the child was with him. The court denied her petition.[10]
- In an Illinois case, a father's support obligation was terminated after he proved that his ex-wife had interfered with his visitation to his children and had destroyed his relationship with his son. He also showed that the termination would have no adverse effect on the children because she had sufficient financial resources.[11]
- An Arizona court held that a man was entitled to credit for medical and dental payments he made for his children if he could show that his wife had given her consent to that support.[12]

INCOME WITHHOLDING

Putting an ex-husband in jail for contempt of child support orders should surely induce him to pay what he owes. Once he is released, the memory of jail should also motivate him to make payments faithfully in the future. Contempt, however, is an exertion for the judicial system. It takes time, costs money, and will always be viewed by many judges as a drastic penalty—perhaps too drastic —for failure to pay child support. Although it sends a message of seriousness, a contempt finding cannot guarantee future payments.

In recent years several states, including Connecticut, have broadened and toughened their child support enforcement procedures by authorizing automatic withholding of support payments from the income of fathers who have shown themselves to be irresponsible. In 1983 the Connecticut legislature enacted a law that allows automatic withholding if a father is more than thirty days late in paying child support. During the first full year of experience with this law, we were able to increase child support collections by 15 percent.

New York was a pioneer in automatic withholding; its courts therefore were among the first to hear challenges to this process. In 1979, one father argued that his due process rights were violated by automatic withholding after his failure to make child support payments because his money was taken without a hearing. The court ruled, however, that there was a superior public interest in recovering welfare payments made to those who are in need from the fathers, who are really obligated to pay them.[13] Another New York court established the supremacy of income withholding for child support over other forms of attachment, assignment, or garnishment. Otherwise, the judge declared, private creditors might be satisfied while the taxpayers would be forced to support the absent father's dependents.[14]

Income withholding has much to recommend it as a method of enforcing child support orders. It is established by an easy court process; it guarantees payment of support at predictable times as long as the ex-husband earns any income; it removes from him the weekly or monthly decision about whether to send the child support check; and the experience of states like Connecticut, which have tried it, shows that income withholding works. It raises more money for children and taxpayers.

Those are the reasons that Congress made automatic income withholding the heart of the 1984 Act. Each state must have a law providing that every child support order *issued* or *modified* after October 1, 1985, include a requirement that the father's *wages* be withheld automatically if he owes an amount equal to at least thirty days of support payments. Individual states are free to reduce the triggering mechanism to less than thirty days and to extend the reach of withholding from wages to all forms of income. This potent enforcement tool will be available to mothers whether they use their public child support agency or a private attorney, and whether or not they are welfare recipients.

An attorney for a mother can also use the income-withholding mechanism to obtain money her ex-husband owes her for past-due child support. The debt will be divided by the judge into regular payments to be deducted from the husband's paycheck until the arrearage is cleared.

Once a woman has a withholding provision in her support order, her ex-husband is obliged to make his payments to a state clearing house that monitors his performance. If he fails to make a payment by the time allowed, he will immediately be notified that withholding is about to occur unless he can present a sufficient reason why it should not. If he believes he can, he will receive a hearing and a decision within forty-five days. The 1984 Act makes clear that only mistakes of fact can stop withholding from going into effect. No other issues—such as the amount of the support order or the denial of visitation rights—can be argued at this hearing.

If the father has no good argument against withholding, an order goes to his employer to begin deducting the appropriate amount from his paycheck and to send it to the state clearing house. The employer is required by law to perform this service, but he is given a modest fee for doing so. According to the 1984 Act, the amount deducted must equal the amount of the support order plus the employer's fee, so long as it is within the limits of another federal law (the Consumer Credit Protection Act). Those limits are 60 percent of disposable income for a man without a second family and 50 percent for a man who has remarried. Very few support orders will exceed those limits. When the state clearing house receives the father's check, it pays the money to the mother, if she is not on welfare, or the first $50 monthly to her and the rest to the state if she is.

The 1984 Act requires the states to make child support withholding *the* priority claim. This means that deduction for support must occur before any other money can be taken out by any other creditors of the father even if they have previously placed claims against his wages. Attorneys should utilize income withholding whether they are establishing a new support order or trying to enforce an old one.

While the 1984 Act requires states to adopt only *wage* withholding laws, several states already have gone beyond that to include other forms of income such as bonuses, unemployment compensation, worker's compensation, disability benefits, commissions, and retirement benefits. In those states, the judge issues the order to withhold to the source of the income payment. If a woman's ex-husband is receiving much income of this kind, she or her attorney should check to see whether their state law requires withholding from it. Even if it does not, the lawyer should try to negotiate a voluntary agreement to have support obligations deducted from all income payments. He might want to do that after filing an opening motion for contempt, which should get the ex-husband's attention.

BONDS, LIENS, AND INTERCEPTS

The 1984 Act has also made it mandatory for *all* states to adopt several procedures which have been tried successfully by various states to guarantee that child support is paid. Since the withholding provisions discussed above concern only wages, these additional procedures will be of special benefit to mothers whose ex-husbands have other types of income and whose states do not allow withholding from those other sources.

For example, the 1984 Act orders the states to adopt "procedures which require that an absent parent give security, post a bond, or give some other guarantee to secure payment of overdue support." Where there are now state laws on this subject, they are vague. Their exact use is determined by the creativity of the attorneys and judges involved. For instance, when the initial child support order is set, or in a later action to enforce it, a man may be required to post a *conditional bond* that will be paid to his ex-wife if he has not paid support for a predetermined period of time. Bonding companies, however, have an understandable distaste for selling child support bonds because of the poor payment record of so many fathers. Attorneys and judges will therefore usually have to use their legal authority creatively to obtain other secured agreements to pay.

Liens are claims against real or personal property that prevent the owner from selling the property until those claims are paid. The 1984 Act requires the states to enact procedures allowing liens in cases of overdue child support. Although many states now allow such liens on real property, most will have to enact them for personal property, that is, for anything besides real estate that a person owns.

Like all the other enforcement mechanisms we have discussed, liens are best used preventively by attorneys in the initial child support agreement or order. But they are also available after the father has stopped paying. A court finds that there is a debt and places a written notice of the debt on the local land records, warning any buyer that the debt must be satisfied before the property can be sold. A lienholder—usually the mother in child support cases—can force a sale of the property to pay an obligation that has been ignored. Child support liens can be helpful if a father is self-employed or even unemployed but has real estate or personal property.

Child support liens are not automatically a priority. They are effective only as of the time they are filed. Creditors who have already placed liens on a man's property, such as the bank that gave him his mortgage, will collect first. Therefore, if liens are appropriate in a particular case, a lawyer should move quickly to obtain a lien and preempt others who are owed money by the father.

One of the most effective methods of collecting child support is by *intercepting* federal or state tax refunds that are due to an ex-husband. This method can be used only to collect overdue support payments, not to secure current payments. It has been available since 1981 for the federal income tax and some state taxes, but only to welfare recipients. The 1984 Act requires all states to offset state tax refunds against child support debts and to make federal and state tax intercepts available to nonwelfare recipients as well. If a father owes child support and his ex-wife suspects he may be entitled to a refund, she or her attorney should pay the small application fee necessary for the tax intercept program. She may quickly and cheaply receive what she is owed.

The intercept program works very simply. Each state's child support enforcement agency submits a list of eligible claims to the Internal Revenue Service and the state tax department, which is then run, usually by computer, alongside the list of those who have tax refunds owed to them. A connection between the two lists results in payment from the refund money of as much as is necessary to satisfy the child support debt. Before payment is made, the father must receive notice that his withheld tax refund money has been intercepted, and he must be given an opportunity to demonstrate some extraordinary reason, such as a mistaken fact, why the intercept should not be completed.

WHAT TO DO IF THE FATHER LEAVES THE STATE

One of the most common ways fathers have found to avoid paying child support is to leave the state and therefore the apparent reach of its courts. The Full Faith and Credit Clause of the Constitution would certainly seem to say that since a child support order is a valid and final judgment of the courts of one state, it must be respected and enforced in the courts of another state. In fact, that conclusion was upheld over fifty years ago by the United States Supreme Court.[15] However, the existence of a legal right does not necessarily mean that it is practically enforceable. The first problem that women have had is locating wayward ex-husbands since, without knowledge of their location, collection of child support is impossible. If a woman was able to find her ex-husband, the second problem has been to afford to retain a lawyer in another state to pursue the delinquent father. Both these problems have now been addressed by federal and state law: the federal and state parent locator services, which were created by the 1974 child support legislation, and the Uniform Reciprocal Enforcement of Support Act, which was adopted by all the states after it was recommended by the American Bar Association in 1950.

A mother seeking to enforce a child support order against a delinquent and absent father will be asked to provide her state's IV-D Child Support Enforcement Agency with whatever identifying information she has on him, preferably a social security number but, failing that, his name and birth date. If the father is thought to be in a particular state, then that state's parent locator service will be notified. Within 60 days, it must begin a search of relevant state information sources including unemployment lists, employment lists, public assistance lists, land records, automobile records, and tax information forms. If the responding state's search fails to produce the whereabouts of the delinquent father, the Federal Parent Locator Service comes into action. It searches comparable federal data sources, including the Internal Revenue Service, the Social Security Administration, the Veterans Administration, the National Personnel Records Center, and the Immigration and Naturalization Service. That vast network of state and local data provides a higher probability of tracking down delinquent fathers than has ever existed before.

Once the out-of-state father is located, the mother turns to the process that URESA created. She begins by filing a petition in the courts of the state where she lives. If the judge finds that the father has a duty to support his children (either because there already is a child support order or because the facts presented suggest that there should be one), he forwards the petition to the state whose courts now have jurisdiction over the father. There, the designated child support enforcement agency notifies the appropriate local prosecuting attorney, who then attempts to locate the father, serves notice on him, and begins to prosecute the case. If successful, he can use all enforcement mechanisms available under the 1984 Act, including automatic wage withholding. The father is given a hearing and may present evidence that he does not actually have a child support obligation or that his obligation is less than is claimed. If he cannot do that, the court is authorized to issue an appropriate support order and take action to force him to pay. His payments are made to the court in the state where the father lives and then sent to the court in the state where the mother and children are. Courts hearing URESA cases have made it clear that they will consider the question of child support only and will ignore peripheral questions such as denial of visitation or child custody.

The Parent Locator Service and the Uniform Reciprocal Enforcement of Support Act can be utilized by a mother who is represented by a private attorney, by a recipient of welfare, or by a nonwelfare recipient who has asked the state's IV-D agency to collect the child support she is owed.

The 1984 Act is a major step away from the traditional state control of family law and toward federalization of the law of child support. In taking that step, the Congress increased interstate uniformity and made it easier for mothers to collect from their ex-husbands who have left the state.

CHAPTER SIX

What Can Be Done to Improve the Child Support System

We are in the midst of a revolution in the American law of child support, but it is unfinished, and that is where concerned individuals and organizations can help. The revolution began with the 1974 federal child support legislation, continued in the tougher enforcement procedures adopted by several states, and reached a new peak in the child support enforcement amendments passed by Congress in 1984. It was stimulated by anger over the multibillion-dollar child support debt that fathers of children on welfare owe to American taxpayers and was strengthened by the insight that poor child support enforcement is feminizing poverty in America and therefore must be a priority item on women's political agenda. The result is that child support law, which had previously been fashioned, like all of family law, largely at the state level, is now dominated by federal standards that have brought a high degree of uniformity of practice throughout the country. The result has been an array of increasingly strong enforcement tools and public attorneys who are charged with the responsibility for using them on behalf of mothers who are not receiving welfare just as much as for the taxpayers and for mothers who are welfare recipients.

These changes of law have been catalyzed in recent years by grass-roots groups of mothers who are not receiving the child support payments they are owed and have banded together to do something about it. Many of these groups have memorable acronyms, such as PECOS (Parents Enforcing Court Ordered Support) in Connecticut, KINDER (Kids in Need Deserve Equal Rights) in Michigan, MUSCLE (Mothers United for Support for Children's Legislative Efforts) in Massachusetts, and POSE (Parents Organization for Support Enforcement) in California. They counsel other mothers, lobby their state and federal legislators, and monitor the behavior of their state judges. Their great accomplishment has been to convince lawmakers that the child support problem is real and serious and that taxpayers, mothers, and children are genuine victims of it. Joining such a group or forming one is one good way to help advance the child support law revolution. There are other vehicles for involvement and action, including local bar associations, women's groups, child advocacy organizations, taxpayers' associations, and political parties. People can even have some effect by acting alone in letters to legislators and newspapers.

What is left to be done? People can monitor their state's adherence to the 1984 federal act, convince their state legislature to adopt additional legislation, and watch their judges to be certain that they are taking child support cases seriously and enforcing the tough laws that are now on the books.

MONITORING THE 1984 ACT

The 1984 Act required that each state adopt several specific improvements in child support law by October 1, 1985, or lose a percentage of the federal reimbursement of its AFDC program. Since that is a multimillion-dollar threat, most states have obeyed. But the requirements of the federal law are vaguely stated in some respects and incomplete in others. Therefore, a state may satisfy the 1984 Act but still leave much to be done.

For example, the federal law requires automatic withholding of wages when a father falls behind in his support payments but does not include withholding from other forms of income, as an ideal state statute should. The federal law also asks states to adopt "procedures under which liens are imposed against real and personal property for amounts of overdue support." That language leaves much room for local judgments about when a lien can take effect, how long it will be effective, and whether any property is exempt from it.

The 1984 Act requires states to divulge information about a father's child support arrears to a credit reporting agency that asks for it, but states have the option of not disclosing overdue payments of less than $1,000.

One of the most important parts of the 1984 Act makes governmental child support enforcement services, including automatic tax intercepts, available to nonwelfare mothers as well as to welfare mothers. People who want to improve child support collection should check to make sure that this is so in their state and that the fees charged, the speed with which cases are processed, and the publicity given to the availability of these services are comparable for nonwelfare and welfare mothers.

In monitoring a state's implementation of the 1984 Act, concerned individual citizens will not be alone. The act itself required each governor to appoint a commission to study some of the questions that Congress was not able to resolve, including interstate enforcement, visitation, and the need for additional legislation.

The most far-reaching topic that must be studied by the state commissions is whether to establish uniform child support guidelines. I have shown in chapter 2 how most child support awards are inadequate to meet the costs of child rearing and that mothers therefore lose out because they must somehow meet the unmet costs. No matter how effective child support enforcement is, mothers and children will continue to suffer unless the underlying support award is adequate. I have also shown how mothers and fathers in very similar circumstances are ordered to pay widely different amounts of child support, presumably because of the subjective evaluation of the particular judge who heard their case.

Uniform child support guidelines can help alleviate both of these inequities. States have until October 1, 1987, to put these in place, so there is time for individuals and associations to get involved.

They can begin by urging their state's child support commission to hold public hearings and accept public input before reaching its conclusions on this critical question.

There is one other vaguely stated provision of the 1984 Act that can bring dramatic changes. It requires states to adopt "expedited processes . . . for obtaining and enforcing support orders" and makes it clear that these new processes may be judicial or administrative. The establishment and enforcement of support orders have traditionally been the work of judges and courts, not administrative agencies. But the chronic congestion of American courts has brought delays in processing child support cases. Some critics also believe that the adversarial nature of our judicial system makes courts the wrong place to settle disagreements over child support, which, as noted in chapter 2, are usually part of larger emotional conflicts between divorcing or divorced parents. Therefore, a less adversarial process for establishing and enforcing child support awards has been suggested by some. Others have argued for administrative handling of child support because they believe it will cost less than the judicial system.

If states prefer to keep child support matters within the judiciary, they must as least expedite the process by providing for masters or referees who will hear child support cases in place of judges and presumably will move them along more quickly. Several states, including Rhode Island and Wisconsin, are already trying this approach.

Either approach—quasi-judicial or administrative—will be an improvement over the existing judicial system. While the administrative option offers the hope of speed and less conflict between the parties, the quasi-judicial option guarantees all the procedural protections the law affords, such as the right to take testimony under oath. State workers' compensation systems give some indication of how an administrative child support agency would function, but there is too little experience with setting and collecting a legal obligation like child support outside the courts to know for certain how it would work. Like so many other important governmental reforms, this one should be tried and evaluated in a few states before it is adopted more widely.

LOBBYING THE LEGISLATURE

The 1984 federal act *required* state legislatures to enact several child support laws and *encouraged* them to adopt even more. Several other laws are suggested by the discussion in this book. The following is a checklist of possible additional legislative action for each state:

* a requirement that all child support awards be automatically adjusted each year to reflect changes in the cost of living;
* authorization for the state parent locator service to receive information from all other state agencies, private employers, and regulated industries, such as banks and utilities;
* an automatic assignment, by law, of child support rights by welfare recipients without their having to fill out a form;
* a requirement that absent fathers fill out financial statements when their children become welfare recipients and update them annually so that more money can be obtained if their incomes increase;
* a requirement that the state be given notice of any legal action that will have an effect on the amount of support owed by the father of children on welfare, so that the state's interests are not diminished without its knowledge;
* a requirement that the paternity of all children, including those in utero, be established at the time of divorce so that fathers cannot later raise paternity questions to avoid paying child support;
* extending the statute of limitations in paternity cases to eighteen years (as required by the 1984 Act);
* a requirement that if a father's health insurance is available, its benefits be extended to his children as part of the support order (required by the 1984 Act);
* a clarification that the father's obligation to pay child support is separate and unaffected by the mother's breach of any of her responsibilities, including the denial of visitation rights to the father;

- a broadly worded authorization of blood testing for the purposes of establishing paternity so that the newest advances in hematology can be used in state courts to prove fatherhood;
- an adequate annual budget for the state's child support agency.

WATCHING THE JUDGES

I have said that child support law is ultimately the work of individual judges who make decisions about how large an award is to be, whether it should be modified, and how it should be enforced. The past failure of our child support system is in good part the failure of judges. They have too often established support awards based more on their estimate of demands on the father than of the needs of the children. When fathers stopped paying even these inadequate awards, judges have often failed to view the offense seriously, rarely utilizing the tools the law provides to guarantee payment or punish delinquency.

This dismal judicial record and the lethargic pace at which so many courts move are the reasons why so many of the recent reforms in child support law have the purpose of restricting judicial latitude (for example, automatic wage withholding and uniform support guidelines) or eliminating judicial involvement altogether (creation of an administrative agency to handle child support).

For the foreseeable future, however, judges will probably continue to play a pivotal part in the establishment and enforcement of support orders. Judges should not be lobbied like legislators, but they can be watched. A good judge-watch program will take many hours of volunteer involvement. It should be done on a coordinated basis over an appropriate period of time after notice of it has been given to court administrators, so that the conclusions of the judge-watchers are based on fact and will be respected. If the monitors conclude that a given judge is not enforcing the child support laws or is consistently biased in his awards, they should complain in writing or in person to their state's chief court administrator. If their state's judges are elected, the court-watchers should distribute a report on the judges' handling of child support cases during their campaigns. If they are appointed, they should testify in their legislative confirmation hearings.

The court-watchers should pay particular attention to whether their judges jail fathers who are in contempt of child support orders. David Chambers, in his study of Michigan's child support laws, concluded that the willingness of judges to jail fathers who do not pay child support had a remarkable effect on compliance with child support orders. Most of those who were jailed found a way to pay their support obligation and therefore buy their way out of jail. For fathers in Genesee County, Michigan, where jailing occurred most frequently, fear of incarceration induced much higher rates of payment, especially when combined with a self-starting, automatic enforcement mechanism. Chambers concluded that "there are few groups so unable to pay that the threat of jail does not produce substantial additional benefits."[1] In fact Michigan has the highest rate of compliance with child support orders of any state in the country.

We have seen in chapter 2 that many fathers do not pay child support simply because they do not want to. We know that paternal neglect of child support awards represents the most widespread disrespect for court orders in America today. Selective jailing for contempt of these court orders should therefore be part of the comprehensive system I have described to guarantee an end to the American disgrace of child support delinquency.

APPENDIX A

State Child Support Enforcement Offices

Alabama

Director
Division of Child Support Activities
Bureau of Public Assistance
State Department of Pensions and Security
64 North Union Street
Montgomery, Alabama 36130
(205) 261-2872

Alaska

Administrator
Child Support Enforcement Agency
Department of Revenue
201 East 9th Avenue, Room 302
Anchorage, Alaska 99501
(907) 276-3441

Arizona

Program Administrator
Child Support Enforcement
  Administration
Department of Economic Security
P.O. Box 6123—Site Code 966C
Phoenix, Arizona 85005
(602) 255-3465

Arkansas

Director
Office of Child Support Enforcement
Arkansas Social Services
P.O. Box 3358
Little Rock, Arkansas 72203
(501) 371-2464

California

Chief
Child Support Program Management
  Branch
Department of Social Services
744 P Street
Sacramento, California 95814
(916) 323-8994

Colorado

Director
Division of Child Support Enforcement
Department of Social Services
1575 Sherman Street—Room 423
Denver, Colorado 80203
(303) 866-2422 (866-5000 general
  information)

Connecticut

Director
Child Support Division
Department of Human Resources
110 Bartholemew Avenue
Hartford, Connecticut 06115
(203) 566-3053

Delaware

Chief
Bureau of Child Support Enforcement
Department of Health & Social Services
P.O. Box 904
New Castle, Delaware 19720
(302) 571-3620

District of Columbia

Chief
Office of Paternity and Child Support
Department of Human Services
425 I Street, N.W., 3rd Floor
Washington, D.C. 20001
(202) 724-5610

Florida

Director
Office of Child Support Enforcement
Department of Health & Rehabilitative
  Services
1317 Winewood Boulevard
Tallahassee, Florida 32301
(904) 488-9900

Georgia

Director
Office of Child Support Recovery
State Department of Human Resources
P.O. Box 80000
Atlanta, Georgia 30357
(404) 894-5194

Guam

Supervisor
Child Support Enforcement Unit
Department of Public Health & Social
  Services
Government of Guam
P.O. Box 2816
Agana, Guam 96910
(671) 734-2947

Hawaii

Director
Child Support Enforcement Agency
Suite 606
770 Kapiolani Boulevard
Honolulu, Hawaii 96813
(808) 548-5779

Idaho

Chief
Bureau of Child Support Enforcement

Department of Health and Welfare
Statehouse Mail
Boise, Idaho 83720
(208) 334-4422

Illinois

Chief
Bureau of Child Support
Department of Public Aid
316 South Second Street
Springfield, Illinois 62762
(217) 782-1366

Indiana

Director
Child Support Enforcement Division
State Department of Public Welfare
141 S. Meridian Street, 4th Floor
Indianapolis, Indiana 46225
(317) 232-4894

Iowa

Director
Child Support Recovery Unit
Iowa Department of Social Services
Hoover Building—1st Floor
Des Moines, Iowa 50319
(515) 281-5580

Kansas

Administrator
Child Support Enforcement Program
Department of Social & Rehabilitation
  Services
2700 West Sixth
1st Floor, Perry Building
Topeka, Kansas 66606
(913) 296-3237

Kentucky

Director
Division of Child Support Enforcement
Department of Social Insurance
Cabinet for Human Resources
275 East Main Street, 6th Floor East
Frankfort, Kentucky 40621
(502) 564-2285

Louisiana

Director
Support Enforcement Services
Post Office Box 44276
Baton Rouge, Louisiana 70804
(504) 342-4780

Maine

Director
Support Enforcement and Location Unit
Bureau of Social Welfare
Department of Human Services
State House, Station 11
Augusta, Maine 04333
(207) 289-2886

Maryland

Executive Director
Child Support Enforcement
    Administration
Department of Human Resources
300 West Preston Street, 5th Floor
Baltimore, Maryland 21201
(301) 383-4773

Massachusetts

Director
Child Support Enforcement Unit
Department of Public Welfare
600 Washington Street
Boston, Massachusetts 02111
(617) 727-7177

Michigan

Director
Office of Child Support
Department of Social Services
300 South Capitol Avenue—Suite 621
Lansing, Michigan 48909
(517) 373-7570

Minnesota

Director
Office of Child Support
Department of Human Services
Space Center Building
444 Lafayette Road

St. Paul, Minnesota 55101
(612) 296-2499

Mississippi

Director
Child Support Division
State Department of Public Welfare
P.O. Box 352
515 E. Amite Street
Jackson, Mississippi 39205
(601) 354-0341, ext. 503

Missouri

Administrator
Child Support Enforcement Unit
Division of Family Services
Department of Social Services
P.O. Box 88
Jefferson City, Missouri 65103
(314) 751-4301

Montana

Director
Investigation & Enforcement Bureau
Department of Revenue
Legal & Enforcement Division
Sam Mitchell Building—Room 465
Helena, Montana 59620
(406) 444-2846

Nebraska

Administrator
Child Support Enforcement Office
Department of Social Services
P.O. Box 95026
Lincoln, Nebraska 68509
(402) 471-3121, ext. 221

Nevada

Chief
Child Support Enforcement
Nevada State Welfare Division
Department of Human Resources
430 Jeanell Drive
Carson City, Nevada 89710
(702) 885-4744

New Hampshire

Administrator
Office of Child Support Enforcement
  Services
Division of Welfare
Health and Welfare Buidling
Hazen Drive
Concord, New Hampshire 03301
(603) 271-4426

New Jersey

Director
Child Support and Paternity Unit
Department of Human Services
CN 716
Trenton, New Jersey 08625
(609) 633-6268

New Mexico

Chief
Child Support Enforcement Bureau
Department of Human Services
P.O. Box 2348—PERA Building
Santa Fe, New Mexico 87503
(505) 827-4230

New York

Director
Office of Child Support Enforcement
New York State Department of Social
  Services
P.O. Box 14, 1 Commerce Plaza
Albany, New York 12260
(518) 474-9081

North Carolina

Chief
Child Support Enforcement Section
Division of Social Services
Department of Human Resources
433 N. Harrington Street
Raleigh, North Carolina 27603-1393
(919) 733-4120

North Dakota

Administrator
Child Support Enforcement Agency

North Dakota Department of Human
  Services
State Capitol
Bismarck, North Dakota 58505
(701) 224-3582

Ohio

Chief
Bureau of Child Support
Ohio Department of Human Services
State Office Tower
30 East Broad Street—31st Floor
Columbus, Ohio 43215
(614) 466-3233

Oklahoma

Administrator
Attention: Division of Child Support
Department of Human Services
P.O. Box 25352
Oklahoma City, Oklahoma 73125
(405) 424-5871

Oregon

Director
Child Support Program
Department of Human Resources
Adult and Family Services Division
P.O. Box 14506
Salem, Oregon 97309
(503) 378-6093

Pennsylvania

Director
Child Support Programs
Bureau of Claim Settlement
Department of Public Welfare
P.O. Box 8018
Harrisburg, Pennsylvania 17105
(717) 783-1779

Puerto Rico

Director
Child Support Enforcement Program
Department of Social Services
P.O. Box 11398, Fernandez Juncos
  Station

Santurce, Puerto Rico 00910
(809) 722-4731

Rhode Island
Chief Supervisor
Bureau of Family Support
Department of Social & Rehabilitative
  Services
77 Dorance Street
Providence, Rhode Island 02903
(401) 277-2409

South Carolina
Director
Division of Child Support
Public Assistance Division
Bureau of Public Asst. & Field Operations
Department of Social Services
P.O. Box 1520
Columbia, South Carolina 29202
(803) 758-8860

South Dakota
Program Administrator
Office of Child Support Enforcement
Department of Social Services
700 Illinois Street
Pierre, South Dakota 57501-2291
(605) 773-3641

Tennessee
Director
Child Support Services
Department of Human Services
111-19 7th Avenue North—5th Floor
Nashville, Tennessee 37203
(615) 741-1820

Texas
Director
Child Support Enforcement Branch
Texas Department of Human Resources
P.O. Box 2960
Austin, Texas 78769
(512) 450-3011

Utah
Director
Office of Recovery Services

Department of Social Services
P.O. Box 15400
3195 South Main Street
Salt Lake City, Utah 84115
(801) 486-1812

Vermont
Director
Child Support Division
Department of Social Welfare
103 South Main Street
Waterbury, Vermont 05676
(802) 241-2868

Virgin Islands
Director
Paternity & Child Support Program
Department of Law
P.O. Box 1074
Christiansted
St. Croix, Virgin Islands 00820
(809) 773-8240

Virginia
Director
Division of Support Enforcement Program
Department of Social Services
8007 Discovery Drive
Richmond, Virginia 23288
(804) 281-9109

Washington
Chief
Office of Support Enforcement
Department of Social & Health Services
P.O. Box 9162-FU-11
Olympia, Washington 98504
(206) 459-6481

West Virginia
Director
Office of Child Support Enforcement
Department of Human Services
1900 Washington Street, East
Charleston, West Virginia 25305
(304) 348-3780

Wisconsin

Director
Bureau of Child Support
Division of Economic Assistance
18 South Thornton Avenue
Madison, Wisconsin 53708
(608) 266-0528

Wyoming

Director
Child Support Enforcement Section
Div. of Public Assistance & Social
    Services
State Dept. of Health & Social Services
Hathaway Building
Cheyenne, Wyoming 82002
(307) 777-6083

APPENDIX B

Child Support Advocacy Groups

Alabama

Kids in Need Deserve Equal Rights (KINDER)
Judy E. Jennings
337 East Haven Drive
Birmingham, Alabama 35215

Arizona

Organization for Protection of America's Children (OPAC)
April J. Skelton
18501 East Bay Road
Higley, Arizona 85236
(602) 988-3238

Dawn McNeese and Sharon Willis
Tempe, Arizona 85283
(602) 839-2371, 839-9974

Kathy Gaddy
Chandler, Arizona
(602) 899-5056

Shirley Haworth
Glendale, Arizona
(602) 246-7673

Elaine Bonner
Mesa, Arizona
(602) 981-0032

Jessie Jordan
Phoenix, Arizona
(602) 243-3344

Terry Raetz
Scottsdale, Arizona
(602) 990-7743

Arkansas

Help Enforce Laws Providing for Children (Help Children)
Karen Bradford
3401 McCord Drive
N. Little Rock, Arkansas 72116
(501) 753-4420

California

Parents Organization for Support Enforcement (POSE)
Bea Shipman and Charlie Wells
P.O. Box 3035
Bakersfield, California 93385

Single Parent Action Network
Mary Drummond
10560 Colona Road
Rancho Cordova, California 95670
(916) 635-9176

Single Parents United "N" Kids (SPUNK)
Susan Speir
5823 Marna Street
Long Beach, California 90815
(213) 598-9206

Top Priority—Children
Teddy Kieley
P.O. Box 2161
Palm Springs, California 92263
(619) 323-1559

Gloria Allred, President
Barbara Miller, contact person
6380 Wilshire Boulevard

Suite 1404
Los Angeles, California 90048
(213) 653-8087

Rachel Newell
6917 LeHavre Way
Citrus Heights, California 95610
(916) 969-6547, 344-1794

Colorado

Kids in Need Deserve Equal Rights
(KINDER)
Mary Alice Chaffin
5420 Wild Lane
Loveland, Colorado 80537
(303) 663-0949

Connecticut

Parents Enforcing Court Ordered Support
(PECOS)
Patricia Caputo
25 Indian Run
Enfield, Connecticut 06082
(203) 749-0894

District of Columbia

Women's Legal Defense Fund
Clare Harrigan
Suite 400
2000 P Street, N.W.
Washington, DC 20036
(202) 887-0364

Georgia

Coalition to Help Enforce Child Support
Marianne-Rich
3056-A Spring Hill Road
Smyrna, Georgia 30080
(404) 434-6626, 633-9503

Indiana

DeKalb Organization for the Enforcement
of Child Support (DOSE)
Linda L. Foster
P.O. Box 724
Auburn, Indiana 46706
(219) 925-1844

Illinois

Organization for Child Support Action
(OCSA)
Mary Wyse
P.O. Box 504
Villa Park, Illinois 60181
(312) 833-3427

Kansas

League of United Latin American Citizens
(LULAC)
Pete Aguirre
P.O. Box 2032
Garden City, Kansas 67846
(316) 275-0271; or (316) 276-2179

Louisiana

Kids in Need Deserve Equal Rights
(KINDER)
Deborah Dean
P.O. Box 6225
Shreveport, Louisiana 71136

Maryland

Organization for the Enforcement of Child
Support (OECS)
Elaine and William Fromm
119 Nicodemus Road
Reistertown, Maryland 21136
(301) 833-2458

Massachusetts

Massachusetts Child Support Payment
Friends
Donna M. Bigelow
P.O. Box 142
Charlton Depot, Massachusetts 01509
(617) 248-5271

Michigan

Kids in Need Deserve Equal Rights
(KINDER)
Patty Kelly
1525 S. Saginaw Street
Funt, Michigan 48503
(313) 785-7470

Marge Johnson
P.O. Box 40563
Redford, Michigan 48240
(313) 759-4568, 357-0456

Patricia Williams
4152 W. 54th Street
Lot No. 187
Mount Morris, Michigan 48458
(313) 687-0456

Karen Pattison
915 Lizzie Street
Sault Ste. Marie, Michigan 49783
(906) 632-6354

Missouri

Organization for Child Support Action
(OCSA)
Beverly Bohmie
P.O. Box188
High Ridge, Missouri 63049
(314) 376-3843

Nebraska

Child Support Collection Task Force
Nebraska Commission on the Status of
Women
Betty Peterson
P.O. Box 6162
Lincoln, Nebraska 68106

New Jersey

Organization for Child Support Action
(OCSA)
Gudrun Piccicacco
P.O. Box 163
Lakehurst, New Jersey 08733
(201) 349-8423

Judi Richter
P.O. Box 1401
Burlington, New Jersey 08016
(609) 386-6211

Jackie DeLussey
21 Hassemen Avenue
Cherry Hill, New Jersey 08002
(609) 586-6043

New York

For Our Children and Us, Inc. (FOCUS)
Fran Mattera
550 Old Country Road
Hicksville, New York 11801
(516) 433-6633

Helena Vitale
Brooklyn, New York 11204
(212) 232-6335

Separated Persons Living in Transition
(SPLIT)
Virginia Engle
1805 Fifth Avenue
North Bay Shore, New York 11706
(516) 435-0740

Oklahoma

Oklahomans Organized for Child Support
Enforcement
Debi Evans
3518 E. Virgin Place
Tulsa, Oklahoma 74115
(918) 832-1860

Oregon

Children Deserve Support
Gail Esters
150 Kingwood Avenue, NW
Salem, Oregon 97304
(503) 378-7526 work, 393-2344

Pennsylvania

Legal Advocacy for Women (LAW)
Rosemary E. Palmer
5149 Keiner Lane
Pittsburgh, Pennsylvania 15205
(412) 279-4389

South Carolina

Organization for Child Support Action
(OCSA)
Felicia Richards
Route 9, Box 272
Wyatt Drive #10
Spartanburg, South Carolina 29301
(803) 574-6347

Tennessee

Gail Forsythe
Forsythe Road
Route 3, Box 42A
Selmer, Tennessee 38375
(901) 645-6387

Texas

Organization for Child Support Action
  (OCSA)
Deborah Seitzer
24163 Boerne Stage Road
San Antonio, Texas 78255
(512) 698-3354

Virginia

For Our Children's Unpaid Support
  (FOCUS)
Bettianne Walsh
P.O. Box 842
Vienna, Virginia 22180
(703) 860-1123

Virginians Organized in the Interest of
  Children's Entitlement to Support
  (VOICES)
Betty Murphy (state coordinator)
10217 Tamarack Drive
Vienna, Virginia 22180
(703) 281-2146

Notes

PREFACE

1 Child Support Enforcement, 8th Annual Report to Congress, Department of Health and Human Services, Dec. 1983, p. 2.
2 Supra, p. 1.
3 Supra, p. 43.
4 Supra, p. 2.
5 Supra, p. 92.

CHAPTER ONE · CHILD SUPPORT LAWS

1 Sir William Blackstone, *Commentaries on the Law of England in Four Books* (Chicago: Callaghan & Co., 1899), at p. 441.
2 John Barbee Minor, *Institute of Common and Statute Law* (1884), vol. 1, p. 405, quoted in Wade R. Bosley, "Child Support—Protecting the Child's Interests," 4 Family Law Quarterly 230, 232 (1970).
3 *McAllen v McAllen*, 97 Minn. 77, 106 N.W. 100 (1906).
4 *Bazeley v Forder*, 3 Q.B. 559 [1868], quoted in Henry H. Foster, Doris J. Freed, and Millard L. Midonick, "Child Support: The Quick and the Dead," 26 Syracuse Law Review 1157, 1158 (1975).
5 Henry H. Foster and Doris Freed, 11 Family Law Quarterly 321, 341 (1978).
6 Lenore Weitzman and Ruth Dixon, 12 University of California at Davis Law Review 473, 479 (1979).
7 *Krieger v Krieger*, 5 Idaho 301, 81 P.2d 1081 (1938).
8 K. Weiner, 6 Florida State University Law Review 1317, 1318 (1978).
9 *Conway v Dana*, 456 Pa. 536, 318 A.2d 324 (1974).
10 *Comm. ex rel. Wasiolek v Wasiolek*, 251 Pa.Super. 108, 380 A.2d 400 (1977).
11 118 Cong. Rec. 829 (1972).
12 120 Cong. Rec. 38196–38198 (12/4/74).
13 Harry Krause, *Child Support in America: The Legal Perspective* (Charlottesville, Va.: Michie, 1981), p. 284.
14 H. Krause, id., p. 285.
15 Child Support Enforcement, 8th Annual Report to Congress, Department of Health and Human Services, Dec. 1983, pp. 88, 90.
16 *Population Profile of the United States*, U.S. Dept. of Commerce, Bureau of the Census, 1982, No. 130, p. 14.

CHAPTER TWO · THE CURRENT CRISIS IN CHILD SUPPORT

1 *Population Profile of the United States, 1982*, U.S. Department of Commerce, Bureau of the Census, No. 130.
2 K. White and R. Stone, Jr., 10 Family Law Quarterly 75 (1976).
3 Lucy Marsh Yee, 57 Denver Law Journal 21 (1979).
4 "Reports, Proposals, and Rulings," 3 Family Law Reporter 2423, 2425 (1977).
5 L. Weitzman, 8 Family Law Reporter 4037, 4049 (1982).
6 L. Weitzman, 8 Family Law Reporter 4037, 4048 (1982).
7 David Chambers, *Making Father's Pay: The Enforcement of Child Support* (Chicago: University of Chicago Press, 1979).
8 S. Hoffman and J. Holmes, "Husbands, Wives and Divorce, Five Thousand American Families—Patterns of Economic Progress," G. Duncan and J. Morgan, ed. (University of Michigan, 1976).
9 J. Wallerstein and D. Huntington, in *The Parental Child-Support Obligation*, Judith Cassetty, ed. (Lexington, Mass.: Lexington Books, 1983), p. 135.
10 D. Chambers, *Making Fathers Pay*, p. 48.
11 Blanche Bernstein, "Shouldn't Low-Income Fathers Support Their Children?" *The Public Interest*, Winter 1982, pp. 63–64.
12 L. Weitzman, 8 Family Law Reporter 4037, 4047 (1982).
13 J. Wallerstein and D. Huntington, *The Parental Child-Support Obligation*, p. 139.
14 United States Department of Labor, Bureau of Labor Statistics, "Perspectives on Women: A Data Book," Bulletin 2080 (1980).
15 United States Commission on Civil Rights, "A Growing Crisis: Disadvantaged Women and Their Children," May 1983.
16 L. Weitzman, 8 Family Law Reporter 4037, 4051 (1982).
17 U.S. Department of Commerce, Bureau of the Census, "Current Population Reports: Money, Income and Poverty Status of Families in the U.S., 1982," No. 140 (1983).
18 Judith Wallerstein and Joan Kelly, *Surviving the Breakup: How Children and Parents Cope with Divorce* (New York: Basic Books, 1980), p. 25.
19 J. Wallerstein and D. Huntington, *The Parental Child-Support Obligation*, p. 147.
20 J. Wallerstein and D. Huntington, id., p. 149.

CHAPTER THREE · HOW TO AVOID HAVING A CHILD SUPPORT PROBLEM

1 "Reports, Proposals, and Rulings," 3 Family Law Reporter 2423, 2424 (1977).
2 *Heller v Heller*, 38 A.D.2d 526, 326 N.Y.S.2d 939 (1971).
3 *Watson v Watson*, 29 Colo.App. 449, 485 P.2d 919 (1971).
4 *Griffin v Griffin*, 79 A.D.2d 828, 435 N.Y.S.2d 149 (3d Dept., 1980).
5 Homer Clark, *The Law of Domestic Relations* (St. Paul, Minn.: West Publishing, 1968).
6 Connecticut General Statutes § 46b-66.
7 Connecticut General Statutes § 46b-84.
8 *Ondrusek v Ondrusek*, 561 S.W.2d 236 (Tex.Civ.App. 1978).

9 *A.S. v B.S.*, 139 N.J.Super. 366, 354 A.2d 100, affirmed 150 N.J.Super. 122, 374 A.2d 1259 (1977).

10 *Gold v Gold*, 96 Misc.2d 481, 409 N.Y.S.2d 114 (1978).

11 *Weisbaum v Weisbaum*, 2 Conn.App. 270, 477 A.2d 690 (1984).

12 *Klein v Klein*, 413 So.2d 1297 (Fla.App. 1982).

13 *Breisach v Breisach*, 37 Ohio App. 34, 173 N.E. 317 (1930).

14 *Cone v Cone*, 68 So.2d 886 (Fla.S.Ct. 1953).

15 *Rosenblatt v Birnbaum*, 16 N.Y.2d 212, 264 N.Y.S.2d 521, 212 N.E.2d 37 (1965).

16 *Blauner v Blauner*, 60 A.D.2d 215, 400 N.Y.S.2d 335 (1977).

17 National Center for Health Statistics, Monthly Vital Statistics Report, vol. 33, no. 6 supp., September 1984.

18 H. Clark, *The Law of Domestic Relations*, p. 165.

19 *Goodright v Moss*, 2 Comp. 591, 98 Eng. Rep. 1257 (1777).

20 *State ex rel. Worley v Lavender*, 147 W.Va. 803, 131 S.E.2d 752 (1963).

21 *People v Thompson*, 89 Cal.App.3d 193, 152 Cal.Rptr. 193 (1979).

22 "Resolution of HLA Testing of 1000 Paternity Cases Not Excluded By ABO Testing," 16 Journal of Family Law 543 (1977–78).

23 *Shepherd v Shepherd*, 81 Mich.App. 165, 265 N.W.2d 374 (1979).

24 *In re Adoption of Young*, 469 Pa. 141, 364 A.2d 1307 (1976).

25 Connecticut General Statutes § 46b–84(b).

26 The Delaware Child Support Formula: Report to the 132d General Assembly by The Family Court of Delaware, April 15, 1984.

27 Philip Eden, *Estimating Child and Spousal Support* (San Mateo, Calif.: Tech Press, 1977).

28 Jacques Van der Gaag, "On Measuring the Cost of Children," in *Child Support: Technical Papers*, vol. 3, Institute for Research on Poverty, Special Report Series (1982), pp. 1–44.

29 Thomas J. Espenshade, "The Value and Cost of Children," *Population Bulletin* Vol. 32, No. 1 (1977), pp. 2–47.

30 Kansas Statutes Annotated § 60–1610(a).

31 Delaware Code Annotated § 513(7).

32 *Zaransky v Zaransky*, 79 A.D.2d 989, 434 N.Y.S.2d 466 (1981).

33 *Neckman v Neckman*, 298 So.2d 534 (Fla.D.Ct. 1974).

34 *McLean v McLean*, 273 S.C. 571, 257 S.E.2d 751 (1979).

35 Philip Eden, "How Inflation Flaunts the Courts' Orders," 1 Family Advocate 2–5 (1979).

36 *Branstad v Branstad*, 400 N.E.2d 167 (Ind.App. 1980).

37 *In re Marriage of Mahalingam*, 21 Wash.App. 228, 584 P.2d 971 (1978).

38 *In re Marriage of Pratt*, 651 P.2d 456 (Colo.App. 1982).

39 National Institute for Socioeconomic Research, "Review of Literature and Statutory Provisions Relating to the Establishment and Updating of Child Support Awards," prepared for the Office of Child Support Enforcement, January 1984, pp. 43–44.

40 *Carpenter v Carpenter*, 25 N.C.App. 235, 212 S.E.2d 911, cert. den. 287 N.C. 465, 215 S.E.2d 823 (1975).

41 *Yost v Yost*, 143 Neb. 80, 8 N.W.2d 686.

42 *Owens v Owens*, 210 Cal.App.2d 705, 26 Cal.Rptr. 847 (1962).
43 *Willcutts v Willcutts*, 88 Ill.App.3d 813, 419 N.E.2d 1057 (1980).
44 *Hambrick v Prestwood*, 382 So.2d 474 (Miss.S.Ct. 1980).
45 *Heaney v Heaney*, 93 Misc.2d 811, 403 N.Y.S.2d 687 (1978).
46 *Kaplan v Wallshein*, 57 A.D.2d 828, 394 N.Y.S.2d 439 (1977).
47 *French v French*, 128 N.H. 138, 259 A.2d 778 (1969).
48 *Brown v Brown*, 474 A.2d 1168 (Pa.Super. 1984).
49 *Gallo v Gallo*, 184 Conn. 36, 46–47, 440 A.2d 782 (1981); *Broaca v. Broaca*, 181 Conn. 463, 465–66, 435 A.2d 1016 (1980).
50 *Commissioner v Lester*, 366 U.S. 299, 81 S.Ct. 1343, 6 L.Ed.2d 306 (1961).
51 *C.I.R. v Gotthelf*, 407 F.2d 491 (1969).
52 *West v U.S.*, 413 F.2d 294 (1969).
53 *Jack Galin*, TCM 1973-62.
54 *In re Lipman*, 5 Family Law Reporter 2409 (Cal.Ct.App. 1979).
55 *Edwards v Edwards*, 97 Wis.2d 111, 293 N.W.2d 160 (1980).
56 *Whitely v Whitely*, 6 Family Law Reporter 2615 (N.C.App., May 20, 1980).
57 *Nelson v Nelson*, 255 Or. 257, 357 P.2d 536, 89 ALR2d 1 (1960).
58 *Curran v Curran*, 26 Wash.App. 108, 611 P.2d 1350 (1980).
59 *In re Marriage of Wyatt*, 159 Cal.Rptr, 784, 6 Family Law Reporter 2140 (Cal.App. 1979).
60 *Corson v Corson*, 46 Wash.2d 611, 283 P.2d 673 (1955).
61 *Cooper v Cooper*, 59 Ill.App.3d 457, 16 Ill.Dec. 818, 375 N.E.2d 925 (1978).
62 *Raymond v Raymond*, 165 Conn. 735, 345 A.2d 48 (1974).
63 *Commonwealth v Barkert*, 5 Family Law Reporter 2707 (Pa.Super. 1979).
64 *Davis v Davis*, 376 So.2d 430 (Fla.D.Ct. 1979).
65 *In re Marriage of Ciganovich*, 61 Cal.App.3d 289, 132 Cal.Rptr. 261 (1976).
66 *Brennan v Brennan*, 187 N.J.Super. 351, 454 A.2d 901 (1982).
67 *Berg v Berg*, 116 RI 607, 359 A.2d 354 (1976).
68 *Trahan v Trahan*, 405 So.2d 1160 (La. App. 1981).
69 *Louis v Louis*, 73 Idaho 165, 248 P.2d 1061 (1952).
70 *Hanson v Hanson*, 47 Wash.2d 439, 287 P.2d 879 (1955).
71 *Aura v Aura*, 342 So.2d 1200 (La.App. 1977).
72 *Smith v Smith*, 293 So.2d 767 (Fla.App. 1974).
73 *Larkin v Marshall*, 23 Or.App. 457, 542 P.2d 1036 (1975).
74 *Perry v Perry*, 213 Ga. 847, 102 S.E.2d 534 (1958).
75 *Andler v Andler*, 217 Kan. 538, 538 P.2d 649 (1975).
76 *Lopez v Lopez*, 125 Ariz. 309, 609 P.2d 579 (1980).
77 *McClaskey v McClaskey*, 543 S.W.2d 832 (Mo.App. 1976).
78 *Matter of Marriage of Cope*, 49 Or.App. 301, 619 P.2d 883, affirmed, 291 Or. 412, 631 P.2d 781 (1980).
79 *Finley v Finley*, 81 Ill.2d 317, 410 N.E.2d 12 (1980).
80 *Reffeit v Reffeit*, 419 N.E.2d 999 (Ind.App. 1981); rehearing denied, 423 N.E.2d 673 (1981).
81 *Lewis v Staub*, 95 Ill.App.3d 243, 419 N.E.2d 1223 (1981).
82 *Cole v Cole*, 338 So.2d 152 (La.App. 1976).

83 *Edin v Edin*, 119 N.H. 783, 407 A.2d 828 (1979).
84 Uniform Marriage and Divorce Act § 316(c).
85 Idaho Code § 7-1105 (1979).
86 *Estate of Brown*, 100 Idaho 300, 597 P.2d 23 (1979).
87 *Kujawinski v Kujawinski*, 71 Ill.2d 563, 376 N.E.2d 1382 (1978).
88 *Hill v Matthews*, 76 N.M. 474, 416 P.2d 144 (1966).
89 *In re Westervelt*, 75 Misc.2d 545, 348 N.Y.S.2d 514 (1973).
90 *Creyts v Creyts*, 143 Mich. 375, 106 N.W. 1111 (1906).
91 *Mahaffey v First National Bank*, 231 Miss. 798, 97 So.2d 757 (1957).
92 *Caldwell v Caldwell*, 5 Wis.2d 146, 92 N.W.2d 356 (1958).
93 *Rex v Rex*, 331 Mich. 399, 49 N.W.2d 348 (1951).
94 *Edelman v Edelman*, 65 Wyo. 271, 203 P.2d 952 (1949).
95 *Warner v Warner*, 615 S.W.2d 904 (Tex.Civ.App. 1981).
96 *Comm. ex rel. Magaziner v Magaziner*, 276 Pa.Super. 169, 419 A.2d 149 (1980).
97 *Dehm v Dehm*, 545 P.2d 525 (Utah S.Ct. 1976).
98 *Crook v Crook*, 80 Ariz. 275, 296 P.2d 951 (1956).
99 *Thomas v Thomas*, 46 Tenn.App. 572, 330 S.W.2d 583 (1959).
100 *Meyer v Meyer*, 493 S.W.2d 42 (Mo.App. 1973).

CHAPTER FOUR · HOW TO CHANGE A CHILD SUPPORT AWARD

1 *Lepis v Lepis*, 83 N.J. 139, 416 A.2d 45 (1980).
2 *White v White*, 141 Vt. 499, 450 A.2d 1108 (1982).
3 Uniform Marriage and Divorce Act § 316 (1979).
4 Connecticut General Statutes § 46b–86a.
5 *Daniels v Daniels*, 38 Ill.App.3d 697, 348 N.E.2d 259 (1976); *Swanson v Swanson*, 51 Ill.App.3d 999, 367 N.E.2d 512 (1977).
6 *Holt v Holt*, 620 S.W.2d 650 (Tex.Civ.App. 1981).
7 *Petersen v Petersen*, 392 So.2d 298 (Fla.App. 1980).
8 *Beck v Jaeger*, 124 Ariz. 316, 604 P.2d 18 (1979).
9 *Flowers v Flowers*, 622 S.W.2d 414 (Mo.App. 1981).
10 *Poehnelt v Poehnelt*, 94 Wis.2d 640, 289 N.W.2d 296 (1980).
11 *Shaw v Shaw*, 138 N.J.Super. 436, 351 A.2d 374 (1976).
12 *Absher v LaCombe*, 432 A.2d 1241 (Maine 1981).
13 *Killinger v Killinger*, 40 Ill.App.3d 962, 353 N.E.2d 284 (1976).
14 *In re Marriage of Goodrich*, 622 S.W.2d 411 (Mo.App. 1981).
15 *Gallo v Gallo*, 184 Conn. 36, 46–47, 440 A.2d 782 (1981).
16 *Spingola v Spingola*, 93 N.M. 598, 603 P.2d 708 (1979).
17 *Moody v Moody*, 22 Or.App. 121, 538 P.2d 82 (1975).
18 *State ex rel. Krueger v Krueger*, 292 N.W.2d 60 (N.D. 1980).
19 *Pendexter v Pendexter*, 363 A.2d 743 (Maine 1976).
20 *Hagbloom v Hagbloom*, 71 Mich.App. 257, 247 N.W.2d 373 (1976).
21 *Hughes v Hughes*, 666 P.2d 739 (Mont. 1983).
22 *Burdock v Burdock*, 5 Family Law Reporter 2675 (Fla.App. 1979).
23 *Curley v Curley*, 5 Family Law Reporter 2246 (Alaska S.Ct. 1979).

24 *Deaton v Deaton*, 393 So.2d 408 (La.App. 1980).
25 *Broday v Broday*, 43 Ill.App.3d 628, 357 N.E.2d 128 (1976).
26 *MacAyeal v MacAyeal*, 575 S.W.2d 626 (Tex.Civ.App. 1978).
27 *Wood v Wood*, 407 A.2d 282 (Maine 1979).
28 *Copeland v Copeland*, 109 Mich.App. 683, 311 N.W.2d 452 (1981).
29 *Black v Bassett*, 619 S.W.2d 193 (Tex.Civ.App. 1981).

CHAPTER FIVE · HOW TO COLLECT CHILD SUPPORT FROM A DELINQUENT FATHER

1 *Panganipabn v Panganipabn*, 396 So.2d 1156 (Fla.App. 1981).
2 *Davidson v Van Lengen*, 266 N.W.2d 436, 5 ALR4th 1001 (Iowa 1978).
3 *Carey v Carey*, 29 Colo.App. 328, 486 P.2d 38 (1974).
4 *Burgin v Burgin*, 195 Ind. 601, 146 N.E. 328 (1925).
5 *Ex Parte Roberts*, 582 S.W.2d 910 (Tex.Civ.App. 1979).
6 *Ex Parte Almendarez*, 621 S.W.2d 664 (Tex.Civ.App. 1981).
7 *Armstrong v Green*, 260 Ala. 39, 60 So.2d 834 (1953).
8 *Mooty v Mooty*, 131 Fla. 151, 179 So. 155 (1938).
9 *Bradford v Futrell*, 225 Md. 512, 171 A.2d 493 (1961).
10 *Headley v Headley*, 277 Ala. 464, 172 So.2d 29 (1965).
11 *Cooper v Cooper*, 59 Ill.App.3d 457, 375 N.E.2d 925 (1978).
12 *Lopez v Lopez*, 125 Ariz. 309, 609 P.2d 579 (1980).
13 *Commissioner of Social Services v Roberto G.*, 72 A.D.2d 9, 423 N.Y.S.2d 155 (1971).
14 *Liedka v Liedka*, 101 Misc.2d 305, 423 N.Y.S.2d 788 (1979).
15 *Yarborough v Yarborough*, 290 U.S. 202, 212–13, 52 S.Ct. 181, 78 L.E. 269 (1931).

CHAPTER SIX · WHAT CAN BE DONE TO IMPROVE THE CHILD SUPPORT SYSTEM

1 D. Chambers, *Making Fathers Pay*, pp. 118–19.

Index